'Mark's business track record speaks for itself! What is nice about his book is it shows the really important things about mind power so that you will be able to emulate his success. Keep it with you and read it over and over again!'
Ron G Holland, Author of *Talk & Grow Rich,* **www.wealth.co.uk**

'Mark Rhodes has given NLP a new look within coaching. I recommend it to NLPers everywhere and to those of us always trying to help others to get to the best living has to offer.'
Dr Richard Bandler, Co founder of the field of NLP, Author of *The Secrets of Being Happy* **& dozens of books and CDs, www.richardbandler.com**

'This book demonstrates the old adage that "if you think you can, you can". By explaining our inbuilt fears and how we can overcome them, it reinforces the will to win and spells out the reasons for failure. Written in a conversational and engaging style, it's the perfect antidote to negativity and a powerful reminder that attitude changes everything.'
Guy Rigby, Director – Head of Entrepreneurs, Smith & Williamson Limited, and Author of *From Vision to Exit,* **www.guyrigby.com**

'As a Certified Financial Planner, Mark helped me to understand my value, what motivated me and enabled me to stop procrastinating! I then developed a unique method of providing financial life coaching, the feedback from my clients has been fantastic and they feel that I am at one with their aspirations.'
Geoff O'Shea, CFP dipPFS Accumulus Consulting

'I met Mark and read his excellent book shortly thereafter. I put his methods into practice and this led directly to me being able to secure a meeting with one of the UK's leading and best-known entrepreneurs!'
Simon Chadwick, Chadwick Nott Legal Recruitment

'Michael Jackson once said "If you want to make the world a better place, take a look at yourself and make a change!" Mark Rhodes is a glowing example of how people can make small changes within their own lives and make a huge difference to their own success. A very honest, open and believable character, Mark has transformed my limiting beliefs about myself and my business and helped me evaluate everything I do and question how I do it. I now have unshakeable belief in myself, my business and my future. "Mark Rhodes has been there and done it, so why not let him help you do it too!"'
James Leighton, Forever Living Distributor

'If you are thinking how great it would be to be successful, focused and happy, then it is time to read this book!'
Julian Evans, Managing Director, Walltastic

Think Your Way to Success

How to Develop a
Winning Mindset and Achieve
Amazing Results

Mark Rhodes

CAPSTONE

This edition first published 2012
© 2012 Mark Rhodes

Registered office
Capstone Publishing Ltd. (A Wiley Company), John Wiley and Sons Ltd, The
Atrium, Southern Gate, Chichester, West Sussex, PO19 8SQ, United Kingdom

For details of our global editorial offices, for customer services and for information
about how to apply for permission to reuse the copyright material in this book
please see our website at www.wiley.com.

The right of the author to be identified as the author of this work has been asserted
in accordance with the Copyright, Designs and Patents Act 1988.

Wiley publishes in a variety of print and electronic formats and by print-on-
demand. Some material included with standard print versions of this book may not
be included in e-books or in print-on-demand. If this book refers to media such as a
CD or DVD that is not included in the version you purchased, you may download
this material at http://booksupport.wiley.com. For more information about Wiley
products, visit www.wiley.com.

Designations used by companies to distinguish their products are often claimed as
trademarks. All brand names and product names used in this book are trade names,
service marks, trademarks or registered trademarks of their respective owners. The
publisher is not associated with any product or vendor mentioned in this book. This
publication is designed to provide accurate and authoritative information in regard
to the subject matter covered. It is sold on the understanding that the publisher is
not engaged in rendering professional services. If professional advice or other expert
assistance is required, the services of a competent professional should be sought.

Library of Congress Cataloging-in-Publication Data
Rhodes, Mark, 1966–
    Think your way to success : how to develop a winning mindset and achieve
amazing results / by Mark Rhodes.
        p. cm.
    Includes index.
    ISBN 978-0-85708-315-9
1. Success. 2. Success in business. I. Title.
    BF637.S8R4447 2012
    650.1–dc23
                          2012006662

A catalogue record for this book is available from the British Library.

ISBN 978–0–857–08315–9 (pbk) ISBN 978–0–857–08330–2 (ebk)
ISBN 978–0–857–08331–9 (ebk) ISBN 978–0–857–08332–6 (ebk)

Set in 11.5/15 pt Adobe Caslon Pro-Regular by Toppan Best-set Premedia Limited
Printed in Great Britain by TJ International Ltd, Padstow, Cornwall, UK

This, my first book, is dedicated to my mother, Joan Sally Florence Rhodes; who sadly passed away in 2009 without suffering but also without warning.

I know a lot of what I have achieved to date, and will go on to achieve in the future, is down to a few beliefs that my mother gave me one of which was:

"You can do anything you put your mind to."

Contents

8.   Strategies (or The Way We Think about Things)   91
9.   Visualizing for Success   109
10. The Comfort Zone   119
11. Inner Critic to Inner Coach   131
12. The Power of Thoughts   147
13. Final "Thoughts"   153

How I Became Successful – Mark's Story   *161*
Index   *171*

Acknowledgements

As you will read in this book, there came a point in my career when I wanted to change from accounting to computers, and that very transition happened as a result of Maurice Hobbs-Hurrell, who as financial director of a London-based company gave me the break to start that transition by hiring me. We both ended up being made redundant from that company, and Maurice was instrumental in my transition to becoming freelance by introducing me to my first client. Some years later, Maurice joined my own company in the role of finance director and helped us grow the business until its sale in 2001.

Before there was a business to sell, and back when the business was just a dream, three people changed everything for me when they backed my idea to start my own software company and gave me the first sales order – they were Mike Ward, Clive Bruce and Peter Cartwright. However, this wouldn't have happened had it not been for Allan Bell backing the idea of having me involved as a consultant in the first place during the previous year.

Funnily enough, after selling the company, and before I'd even realized a future in speaking existed for me, it was Mike Ward who gave me that first break into speaking, at one of his conferences. I also worked with Mike on a consulting basis at Phoenix Trading, a business owned by Mike, Robin Bradley and Sheila Shaw.

Way back before any of this though, thanks must go to my parents for somehow managing to achieve the balance of creating an environment in which I wanted to be successful without ever putting any pressure on me to succeed.

At the time of writing this in 2012, Jacqueline and I have been married for seventeen years and our children Holly and James are twelve and seven respectively. They, of course, need a big thank you for understanding the times I had to travel on business and the hours I sometimes had to work in order to get where we wanted to be.

About the Author

Author photo by Peter Evans Photography (www.peterevansphoto.com)

Mark Rhodes is an entrepreneur, mentor, international speaker and trainer in success who shows people how to massively improve their results with little or no extra effort!

Mark empowers individuals in their life, careers and business. He has also "been there and done it" – from the ground up, he started, built and ran his own Internet Software company, which he then sold to a USA Silicon Valley organization in 2001. This was just two years after starting the business in 1999. Mark's clients included top brand names such as The Body Shop at home, Virgin Cosmetics and Dorling Kindersley Publishers.

On selling his company, Mark retired at the age of thirty-five, but only for fifteen minutes before he got bored!

Mark was keen to figure out how he had become successful and now spends his time teaching others, so that they can achieve their own dreams. Mark's focus is on what he believes to be one of the most crucial aspects of whether someone achieves success or not, their "success mindset", as well as the business specific topics of "winning more sales" and "exceeding goals" – because of the simple fact that most people don't set a big enough goal!

In addition to speaking at conferences and events, Mark is a trainer and mentor for people that want to succeed. Mark makes everything so easy to understand and implement. His natural down-to-earth style and the fact that he teaches the exact same tools and techniques that he uses everyday in his own life is a refreshing change.

Mark speaks internationally for many types of businesses at both conferences and internal staff development events. For more information, go to Mark's website at www.rhodes2success.com where you can find out about his speaking engagements and sign up for his regular newsletter of "Success and Personal Development", and find out about events where Mark is speaking live and details of his online Webinars.

There are also details on the website about Mark as a speaker and business mentor around the world and how to get in touch with him.

Foreword

It is a great pleasure to provide a foreword to Mark Rhodes' new book, for two reasons. Firstly, I have known Mark for several years and have seen the passion of his work in action. As a business mentor, he walks his talk and has the ability to awaken peoples' self-belief. Mark is generous with his time and with his knowledge and is motivated by a desire to help others succeed. His approach is personal, supportive and collaborative and I know that there are hundreds of business owners who are more focused and more successful today because of the help he has given them. This authentic and warm approach comes across on every page of his book and his coaching style will offer support to all those who know that they need to alter their mindset in order to make things happen.

Think Your Way to Success is based on Mark's own experiences in life and business and his knowledge of NLP. However, you do not need any knowledge of NLP in order to gain full benefit from the book.

Secondly, I have great belief in the positive impact of NLP and I welcome Mark's focused and clear guide to how NLP techniques can help everyone to develop a mindset for success. As CEO of The Coaching Academy I have seen time and again how the power of self-belief makes the crucial difference between action and inaction. When the going gets tough or the small voice of self-doubt raises its head, it is always mind over matter that matters most.

In *Think Your Way to Success*, Mark gives both individuals and business owners the benefit of his experience and demonstrates how everyone can use simple, powerful techniques to make their dreams become reality. He is on a mission to transform people's lives and give them the tools to turn 'I can't' into 'I can'. If you want to stop 'tiptoeing' through your life and start striding through it with confidence, taking some time to read and follow the advice in Mark's book will be an excellent way to start.

Bev James
CEO of The Coaching Academy and
Best Selling author of *Do It! or Ditch It*
www.bevjames.com

INTRODUCTION

In Part One, we're going to look at success: setting and achieving goals from a personal development point of view. We'll look at how successful people think and how we can easily adopt their ways of thinking if we apply our minds in the correct way. A big part of the goals process is thinking about the goal in the correct way, a way in which the most powerful parts of your mind can engage and make things happen for you.

In Part Two, we look at why we have certain fears that hold us back from taking the action we need to take, how fear works and how we can change it so we get on with the things that need to be done.

Next, we'll look at how the brain manages experiences. We'll look at how fears and phobias develop, and how we actually build perceptions from an early age of how we think we fit into the world, what we mean in the world and what other people mean to us.

Then we'll move on to look at strategies and how to visualize success, such that you do get results, especially when you understand not only how to do this properly but how it works as well.

Strategies are basically how we do things in life, and the way we think about things, how we act on them, and how we actually go ahead and take action.

Then we'll look at "comfort zones" and "fear". We won't dwell on fear for too long because it isn't a really popular subject with people – even though most of us do "fear" very well!

We'll then take a look at limiting beliefs and what I call the "I can't" virus. This is when people say things like:

"I can't give presentations."
"I can't cold call."
"I can't delegate."
"I can't talk to strangers."

Or "I can't . . . " whatever it is. This is the "I can't" virus.

We'll then touch a bit more on the "power of thought". We'll talk about thoughts; we all have them all of the time, so they're quite important.

Everything will be summarized with some "final thoughts".

What about Motivation though?

I don't believe that many people lack motivation in its purest form. In my experience, people either haven't got a compelling enough goal or dream they're driven towards, or they have certain fears, hang-ups or beliefs that stop them taking the actions that would lead to that goal or dream becoming a reality in their lives.

Think about it, if you had a compelling goal or dream for your life that when you thought about it you couldn't wait to experience it, and you had no fears or comfort zone issues holding you back from doing what was needed to achieve that dream life, would you need motivating? I don't think so. You would most likely be up out of bed every morning eager to get started on another day of building your dream life.

Most people's reason for not making progress is their "mindset".

Let me give a classic example to illustrate this. In a room, we set up two tables with chairs, telephones and a script to be used for cold calling to other companies about a product we have on offer. We get two people in the room and tell them to make some cold calls. Now one person sits down and starts making the calls, the other runs out the room! No doubt you know which one you'd likely be out of the two.

Now what's the difference between these two people? There can only be one difference: how they're thinking about it – their mindset. One of them is thinking about it in a way that causes them to engage in the action, the other is thinking about it in a way that causes them to run away.

I was sitting in on a workshop when the speaker, Steve Clarke, asked the audience "Who here loves cold calling?" One lady, Hayley Feeley, Managing Director of ChairsGB. com put her hand up and replied "I do, I love it, I just don't get enough time these days." No doubt you'll be surprised by this reaction to something like cold calling. I certainly was.

So I tracked Hayley down at lunch time and reminded her about what had happened that morning. I simply asked her this: "When you make one of those cold calls and the other person either puts the phone down on you or has a go at you and puts the phone down, what do you think?" – you see I wanted to understand her thinking behind this. She turned to me and said "They obviously don't care that much about their own business otherwise they would have listened to me a little while longer to see if I could have added value to what they are doing."

Now most people in that situation wouldn't think like that. They would most likely think either that they shouldn't be doing it or that they were not very good at it.

Like most things in life, what we say we can't do we really wish we could do. We end up saying things in our heads like, "I really wish I could do that," then say, "I can't do that." When you experience this, you want to do it, but you can't, but you know you really want to, and so you have these debates in your head.

Deep down you know that it would be really great if you could; or that if you "were the sort of person" to do that, then you could take your life or success to the next level. Well, you can.

Your mindset is very often the difference between doing something in a way that gets massive results and running away.

In life, I break everything into two areas: skill set and mindset.

Skill Set

This is what you do, how you do it and when you do it. Skill set is pretty much a commodity today, with the Internet; you can go and find out how to do pretty much anything these days, but unless you've got the other element of "mindset" aligned you're unlikely to do very much with the knowledge.

You can have the best business idea in the world but if you stay at home and don't take any action or tell anyone about it you are unlikely to have any success, you need the appropriate mindset to go with that skill set.

Mindset

This is having the belief, the confidence, the motivation and a compelling goal or dream for your future. You probably won't be able to do very much with the skill set alone. This is why, in business or life in general, when we tell people what to do, we show them how to do it – but then they don't go ahead and do it because they're thinking things like:

"Well, it's just not like me to do that."
"I'm not the sort of person that does that."

"It'll seem silly."

"They might say no."

Now to say you lack confidence or belief is not a weak thing because everybody does, all of the time, because as humans we're constantly moving forward and growing. Therefore, if there's anyone in the world that isn't feeling fear and hitting their comfort zone then they just aren't growing. Every time you conquer something and it comes within your comfort zone, you should be moving on to the next level and hitting it again. This is why many people, no matter how successful they are, commit to a regime of ongoing personal development.

Making Success Work for You

One of the problems in the personal development world is that people attend seminars or buy books but don't do anything afterwards.

A lot of people buy a personal development book and don't read it – then they're amazed that they haven't changed! The next group of people are slightly better but still don't get any benefit. They buy the book, they read it, but they don't do anything else. They just put the book on the shelf. We tend to call that "shelf help" as opposed to "self help"!

To make this book work for you, you have to read it, and that's a good start.

But you have to think about what you've read. After every couple of pages, you should stop and consider what you've read, and **you've got to do the things it tells you to do!**

In life, you don't really know anything until you do it. Intellectually you might know it, but until you *actually* do it you don't know it.

I spoke at a big conference where the talk was recorded and made available to attendees as a free download by the organizers. One of the attendees asked me if I would do an all day workshop based in the area he lived. The attendee gave the CD recording to everyone to listen to prior to the workshop. On the CD was an exercise that asked them to sit down for five minutes and write out their dream life for the future.

At the start of the workshop, I asked the audience how many had listened to the CD. It turned out about twenty out of the fifty attendees had listened to it, four had listened to it more than once. When I asked how many completed the five minute exercise, the answer was NONE! So despite liking the CD enough to pay for a full day seminar, not one of them had even bothered to do the single five minute exercise key to the process.

All too often people read a short exercise, understand it and then think they don't have to do it! You don't know it, experience it or understand it until you do it.

This is similar to hearing people respond to personal development material with, "I've heard it all before." Like I said earlier, you may have heard some of it, but are you doing it? There's a big difference between hearing it and doing it.

I'll tell you something, I've presented the material in this book many times and I learn something new every single time I do it. This is because I've changed; I'm a different person to the person who presented the same material last week. If you go back and read a book for the second time, you'll notice things in there you didn't notice before.

Everything you do in life generates thoughts, and thoughts make you who you are. So, if you've read a book, and generated loads of thoughts, your brain has been changed. Therefore, the next time you read it, you've got a different degree of intelligence – you've got a different perception of things.

People often say to me, "You've got it all," but I still get scared; I still lack confidence in some things I do. The only difference between me and a lot of other people is what I've learnt over the years, and it's all about mastering the secret to life . . .

Part One

SUCCESS

1

THE "SECRET" TO LIFE

Your thoughts, whatever you think, generate your feelings or your emotional state, which in turn determines the quality of the actions you take – or whether you take any action at all. A lot of the time that fear raises its head, or an uncomfortable feeling emerges, and no action is taken. You don't make that call, or you don't speak to the person you need to speak to. The actions you take – or don't take – in turn determine your results.

Thoughts	⟹	Feelings – how you feel about something
Feelings	⟹	Quality of the action you take or don't take
Action	⟹	Outcomes and results you get
Outcomes	⟹	More thoughts, so around it goes again in the cycle

When you have good thoughts about doing something, you get good feelings, confident feelings, empowering feelings – whatever is appropriate to the thoughts. Then you take more effective action, so you're going to get better results. When you get better results, you're going to have even more good thoughts related to how well you did. It goes on and on like a self-fulfilling prophecy, and then you're in what's often called "the zone". This is the place where everything seems to go right – and I'm sure you've experienced times like this.

But the trouble with this formula is that if you think bad thoughts, you get bad feelings and emotional state, bad quality of action (or no action), bad outcome and results. So if we could all instantly just switch and say, "From now on, I'm just thinking good thoughts," we'd be fixed. Unfortunately, because this subconscious part of the brain that's running on autopilot is involved, people struggle to do this directly or on an ongoing basis.

The alternative is to apply tools and techniques to our way of thinking about the fears that hold us back in certain situations. This is what we're going to be covering as we go through this book.

Once you understand how the brain works, and how it manages experiences, then you can really start to change the way it works for you, and experience things in a whole new way. A new way that starts to create more of what you you'd like in your life and less of what you don't want.

So let's get started.

2

INTRODUCTION TO SUCCESS

When thinking about success, a lot of people will probably think about the financial position they want to reach – how much money they'd like to earn. As you go through the following chapters though, you'll find that it's not all about the money. Sometimes, attaching your goals to something other than the money can actually be more engaging for your brain. This will encourage you to go and search out the goal and, as a result, bring you the money – as an almost "added benefit".

This isn't your typical business goals strategy though. A typical approach to achieving goals in business is very methodical – to do this, this and this. There are all these steps and checkpoints, which will keep you on track to your target. However, for one reason or another, many people find it difficult to stay on their goal-setting course. This is usually because they have the "skill set" aspect of goal-setting but not the "mindset of goals" that engages the mind, especially the most powerful part of the mind, in motivating and driving them towards all the things that, in turn, lead to the desired success.

There are really just a few strategies in the "mindset of goals and success", and they are very different to those you're likely to get in a business goal-planning technique. However, they are strategies that have been proven over hundreds of years and are used over and over again. I've given some of these strategies my own twists over time, incorporating things I've discovered – and use myself – that actually make these simple techniques even easier to use and understand.

There are two real groups of "goal setters". You've got the "business process" types – people who have been very academic, enter into structured careers and go on to receive goal-setting training. Then, quite often, you find there are entrepreneurs, self-employed people or business owners who are likely to say something like, "I had very little educational background at all, but I just knew that I was going to be successful." When you delve into it, and you find out how both groups think, how things turned out the way they did, and how they managed to achieve what they wanted to achieve, you actually discover they've all pretty much followed a very similar process, the "non-business process", i.e. exactly what we're talking about here – the mindset of goals. However, very often those who have followed the structured business process and achieved great success don't realize they are also using a mindset of goals approach, it is just something they have naturally developed.

The business process is fine; it's like many things in life, both processes can work on their own for different people, and you can also do fantastically well by using both the business process and mindset of goals. Don't let this distract you from anything you already do that works, because, for a start, different things work for different people, and some things will work for everybody. Use what you're about to discover here in addition to anything you may currently do that works for you.

You may be amazed to discover that, compared to anything you may have learnt before, when setting goals in the way I'm going to show you, you don't even need to know how you're going to achieve them – yet. You don't even have to know at the moment what steps you'll need to take!

If you set your mind up correctly, to know *what* you're going to go for, then the steps will become apparent as things start to fall into place.

One of the problems with working out all the steps in advance, of course, is that you shut yourself off to other opportunities that come up along the way, outside of the rigid path you've set yourself. You say to yourself, "I'm going to set this goal to become successful; so what I've got to do is go and get clients in this area to get me to this next stage, so I can do this and I can then promote the business like this, and I can then sell the business."

Well, what about if there's an opportunity somewhere else? You're not going to pick up on it if you've programmed your brain in a rigid way. The problem is that the brain is so powerful and – you've probably heard this before – we only use a small part of the brain's full power. The brain is like a super computer running on many programs, and some of these need to be updated and changed.

Most of the brain's power is unconscious, it's the part that's making your heart beat, pumping your blood, doing all that good stuff, and it's that part that's more powerful than your conscious reasoning.

For example, say you're in a situation where you have to get up and talk in front of a group of people, go across a room to talk to a stranger or make a cold call. You may think to yourself: "I want to do that, I want to do that." You convince yourself you're going to do it – whatever it is – and just as you go to do it, fear steps in, and you walk away.

When you get outside later you may well kick yourself, "Why didn't I do that? How stupid was that? I'll do it next time." You go back in, that fear returns, and you walk away again. That fear, that really powerful emotion or feeling of being stuck, is generated by the subconscious, or unconscious, part of the mind. The subconscious part of your brain works hand in hand with emotions. So what you need to do is attach the right emotions to your goals – and I'll explain why and how it works. If you can tap into connecting the right emotion to your goals when you think about them, the brain will realize that goal is relevant to you and open up your awareness to opportunities you perhaps previously won't have noticed.

People say, "I'm never in the right place at the right time", but, as I heard Bob Proctor say once, "We are often in the right place at the right time, we just don't realize it." It's just not in our awareness at the time.

It is said that on average, consciously, we can only track between five and nine things at one time. There are millions of things going on, and our brain discounts what it believes is not relevant to us. This can include your goals or anything that might lead to them if you've not set them properly.

As already mentioned, people pull back from doing things they feel negative about doing, where they experience that fear emotion, and often end up saying they lack confidence.

So, because confidence is such a big issue with most people, before moving further into goals, success and the other exciting areas we should take a little look at confidence. This, more than anything else, is what people tell me is the reason they cannot be more than they currently are.

3

THE
CONFIDENCE
LEVELS

Everyone talks about confidence an awful lot. Confidence really is just your degree of certainty about an outcome or about how you'll behave or feel in a given situation – it's *your* degree of certainty.

It's useful to look at confidence on the following four levels:

1. What You Know You Can't Do

It's possible that you might not set a big enough goal because you may have too many doubts. You might think you'll never get there, or you don't want the disappointment if it doesn't work out. But if you don't set a big enough goal, it won't be attractive enough to pursue. Setting a big enough goal is covered later.

So, the bottom level is "What you know you can't do." Essentially, 99% of the things you say you *can't* do are the things you *won't* do. You could do them, but you won't, and you won't do them usually because of some fear, some limiting belief or some imagined consequence. These can be valid reasons to you at the moment; I'm not looking to dismiss your fear. The important point to grasp is usually it isn't that you *can't* do things it is that you *won't* do them because of . . .

2. What You Think Might Go Wrong

What you think might happen is the next level. This is an interesting one because with this one, you've got to be careful. People think about their goals and hope for success. However, they go through their daily life expecting failure, they expect the other person not to be interested when they go to a meeting, they expect it not to go that well, and expectations have a huge bearing on how things actually turn out.

3. When You Expect a Good Outcome

This next level is the first of two that I call the "manifesting" levels. **When you expect a good outcome** – your expectation is so important. This is the point at which you grow. Let's say two people go into the same sales presentation or meeting; one has an expectation of it going well, the other has an expectation of it going badly. They could say exactly the same things, but the chances are that the optimistic one will get the deal. If you've got an expectation that things will go well, you're going to be enthusiastic, and that enthusiasm is contagious. If *you're* enthusiastic, other people will get enthusiastic and wonder what it's all about. Genuine enthusiasm can't be faked, and that's why you've got to be passionate about what you're doing, you've got to believe in what you're doing if you want to maximize it. You've got to believe in it because otherwise there's always going to be something holding you back.

25

Often, when I ask successful sales people about their strategies for selling they will say to me, "I'm actually no good at selling, but I just love this product."

When you really love something and you're passionate about it, that enthusiasm is contagious, and that's why expectation is important. Even if they say "No", one of your main thoughts is likely to be, "I can't believe they couldn't see the good in it, what is the matter with them?" Or "They obviously don't care enough about their business or lives, otherwise they'd have gone with this!"

A lot of people in a situation where a sale doesn't happen would say, "What's the matter with me? Why didn't they like me? Why didn't they like what I was selling? I've obviously done it wrong, there's no point me being in this game." But if you've got the expectation of a good outcome and that enthusiasm because you're passionate about what you do, it changes everything. If you don't totally believe in or have the enthusiasm for what you do, you've got to ask yourself why, find out why, and go and get those things resolved. Get those things worked out, because they are holding you back.

4. What You Know You Can Do

At the very top level – this is where you have the most confidence, because you know what you can do.

Summary

Level 3 is the powerful level because this is where you're growing in your level of success. Although you don't know 100% that it's going to go well, you've got an expectation of a good outcome, not a guarantee. So Level 3 is the power level because this is where you're growing. If you're not at this level, you're going to risk stopping at level 4, constantly doing what you already know you can do, which is the same thing, same results. Growth comes with a level of the unknown, dropping back a level or more on the confidence tree, gaining new skills and moving each new skill up into what you know you can do raises your level of success and your options for the future.

4

WHAT MAKES A SUCCESSFUL PERSON SUCCESSFUL?

It's useful to think about what makes a person successful, because a lot of the time you might say to yourself that you can't be successful because of your upbringing, your social background, what your parents did, your education, where you live or numerous other reasons. These are really just excuses or limiting beliefs.

If you look at very successful people, people who have achieved really amazing goals, you'll often find that they didn't come from ideal backgrounds. They just knew they wanted to be successful, and set their mindset up in the right way – whether they consciously realized that at the time or not.

So, when you think about your education, social background, successful parents, location, it can be tempting to use these as an excuse to put yourself off your goals. You need to realize, though, that all too often these are excuses and not reasons.

It's not about where you live, what you actually do or where you do it. It's about how you do it and what level you restrict yourself to.

There are lots of self-made people with no formal education at all. For example, Abraham Lincoln had no real education but was apparently one of the best US presidents in history.

Whether you have successful parents or not doesn't determine your success either. Take age as an example as well. All too often you hear of dot com millionaires in their teens and then people like Colonel Sanders of Kentucky Fried Chicken, who I believe was in his sixties when he started his business and had his success.

These small examples show how you can set much bigger goals than you think you are capable of achieving.

So what *is* it that makes a successful person successful?

It's about how they think and set goals. That's what makes people successful – they take action towards their goals. Therefore, it's not just about setting goals; you've got to follow it through with action.

One of the things about this technique I'm going to share with you is that when you program your subconscious mind through using your emotions to set your goals, little internal instincts will crop up. It's different for everyone, but you will get little thoughts or feelings such as: "I don't know why it is, but something tells me that I should do this."

These are internal instincts. You never know where things are going to lead; you never know who you're going to be in a room with, you never know where things are going to take you. When you get these internal instincts or inner prompts and ideas come up, you must take action on them.

Here are the top traits that successful people have, which very often those people who do not achieve success are missing:

1. Enthusiasm and Expectation

Successful people have enthusiasm which can be sensed on an instinctive level. Someone with enthusiasm, and who has our best interests at heart, can be easily spotted. With genuine passion and enthusiasm you become a person that people want to listen to and take notice of, because people want to know more from someone who is enthusiastic. Enthusiasm comes from knowing what you have to offer, or want to tell people about, is something fantastic that is going to add value or enrich someone else's life in some positive way. With this enthusiasm there is no pushy attitude of trying to convince people of your point of view, just an enthusiastic attitude to telling people about what you can do and can offer. With it also comes expectation of a good outcome.

When I started mentoring business owners, I quickly realized a lot of people didn't think about things in the same way I did. Most people I work with in business dread sales meetings or meeting potential clients. Before the meeting they think of all the reasons why it might go wrong, all the reasons why the potential client or customer might not want to do business with them.

With that amount of negativity going on it is near impossible to visualize a winning situation. In fact, it could easily lead to desperation if you really need that deal.

When I owned my company I was so excited and enthusiastic to see new potential clients. I couldn't wait to get there and wow them with what we did and what we could do for companies like them. I went in excited to be there and seeing the deal signed before I had even arrived. In this way so many more deals did get signed off than would have if I had gone in full of negativity and desperation.

2. Confident and Definite

Successful people are also confident and definite about what they can do and this really helps to attract the new customers and clients in.

Take a networking event, for example. If I was at such an event and someone told me they really wanted more success, I could react in a very casual way saying something like "you know what . . . I could probably look at something with you if you want." This comes across a bit vague and so the best I can hope for is the potential client to respond with, "That sounds interesting, give me your card and I will give it some thought." It's highly unlikely I would get much more from this.

However, if instead I immediately and without hesitation say "Well I can definitely help you with that" they are much more likely to fully engage. My prompt and confident statement would cause them to engage at a different level. I am telling them I am the solution and all of a sudden they want to know more. This is all because I was confident and definite in my response when I spotted an opportunity. It is the same thing when a potential customer or client asks you how much your product or service costs.

Any hesitation or stuttering in your response indicates you may not be very comfortable about your price. I was always confident that we were providing amazing value and, therefore, our price wasn't an issue in my mind. If at any stage there was some doubt in my mind I would sit down and prove to myself based on benefits to the clients and savings they may make and compare to other solutions available such that I was sure our prices were, at the end of the day, right, then I would be confident in saying them to my prospects.

3. Reacting and Responding

When something occurs, be that good or bad, a successful person doesn't react or *overreact*. Instead, they *respond*. A response is considered after contemplating the various factors involved in a situation. A reaction tends to be an emotional response created immediately and often without having full information.

For example, most people reading an email that appears to be a complaint will jump on the defensive and immediately send a reply, which all too often can be confrontational and missing all the facts. Too many times I have seen people over react to an email, let loose in their reply only to discover the original message they received has been misinterpreted.

Now, I fell into this trap myself a year ago despite understanding fully about reacting and responding!

My wife and I had gone to parents evening at the school for our son James who was just coming up to six years old at the time. Before going in, we had to sit outside in the hall and look through his work books. All of a sudden I noticed the teacher had written under a piece of his work 1/10, i.e. one out of ten! Poor little boy, I thought, "he's only little, one out of ten what is that going to do for his confidence, you wait till I get in there, I will give that teacher a piece of my mind." I was outraged. Just then, I saw the headmaster approaching down the corridor, well it can be "Mr Rhodes" from now on, I thought, no more "Mark". "Wait till he gets here, I will tell him what I think as well as telling the teacher once we go into the classroom."

Just before the Headmaster reached us, I turned over a few more pages and noticed the teacher had written underneath James's work 15/10. It was at that point that I realized it was the date she was putting on the page!

Clearly, I had reacted (or overreacted) before I had all the information. There is many a time I have had nightmares imagining what would have happened if I hadn't noticed at the last minute. I have visions of me ranting and raving for ages to the teacher and all the time she stands there saying nothing, waiting for me to calm down.

Eventually I calm down and she casually says "It's the date Mr Rhodes." Luckily I had realized just in time. Imagine how bad I would have felt if I had gone in, ranting and raving at the teacher? Regardless of the fact that I had realized just in time though, I should never have been thrown into a reactive state. I should have stayed calm, collected additional information and then considered my position.

A successful person, then, is more likely to stay calm, ask for further details or clarification and only then put together a suitable response.

4. Fear of Failure and Disappointment

One of the major things that differentiate successful people from unsuccessful people is how they think about "failure".

As far as your goal is concerned, you haven't failed if you don't achieve one of the steps first time – or the second or third time. As Napoleon Hill explains in *Think and Grow Rich*, it's an "unplanned outcome".

Failure only exists when you give up and say, "I'm not doing that, I'm not doing that anymore, I can't do that, I can't become whatever, I'm not doing it." That's the point where you fail, when you decide to give up.

Most people think failure is when we don't get a person to say "yes" that day, or we don't achieve a particular target immediately, that is when most people say they have failed. This out-of-date thinking comes from, perhaps, teachers or parents pointing out everything you did wrong, and not focusing more on everything you did right.

The world doesn't work like that. The most successful people are successful because they failed time and time again, but carried on. They found a different approach and a different way of making it work. We do this as children, but most of us won't do it as adults.

My little boy, who's seven at the time of writing this, enjoys playing with his Nintendo DS – the handheld electronic game. He loves it, and has been playing it since he was four years old. When he started he couldn't read the sixty-four-page instruction manual that comes with each game. So he plays around to see what works, and what doesn't work. If he doesn't get the outcome he wants because his little character dies or he loses the race, he does less of that. He carries on and takes a different approach. He does more of what works and less of what doesn't work until he can play the game perfectly and win every time, or at least nearly every time.

He didn't give up on the first, second or third attempt because he's too innocent at that age; he hasn't been programmed by the media, by school and by parents that if you don't get the right outcome, you've failed. He has the mindset at that young age that if he hasn't got the outcome he was looking for, it just means he hasn't figured out the right way yet!

As adults, a lot of us will only have a couple of goes at playing one of these games before throwing it down saying, "What a load of rubbish, I'm not wasting my time on that." We feel embarrassed because we didn't get it right first time. For some reason we expect to be able to do new things right the first time, and if we can't then it must mean it's never meant to be! Somewhere along the line we have forgotten about a learning curve, about adjusting what we do until we get the result we are looking for. All of us were four years old once, so we still have that ability in us to be curious about our results, and do more of what works and less of what doesn't work. Essentially this isn't about learning anything new, it's about unlearning all of the unhelpful things we learnt or started to believe since we were four years old.

So, you need to go back to this way of thinking. Have a go at something, adjust, and keep going through it until you find what works. Then keep doing more of it. It's too easy to get wrapped up in what other people are going to think, or worrying about how disappointed you will be if things don't work out great first time.

Think about this: let's say my goal is to get a new job. I've had five interviews and every one of them has said, "No." This isn't failure.

My goal is to get a new job and the opportunity or possibility for me to get a new job still exists – so I can't have failed. I might need to take some feedback after five "No"s, and ask myself "am I applying for the right positions and saying the right things?" I might need to adopt a different approach to interviews. But, as long as the possibility to achieve my goal on a different day in a different way still exists, then I haven't failed. This is the "unplanned outcome" I mentioned earlier by Napoleon Hill. The most successful people get there by doing it, and if they don't get the outcome they want, they have another attempt or change their approach until they get it right.

Successful people do extraordinary things to get to their goals; they don't get wrapped up in what other people think. Most of the time other people aren't thinking anything anyway, most of the time it's all in our own heads.

One of the biggest differences between those who succeed and those who don't is that the ones with the big success in the end kept going. You will often hear them say, "I always knew one day I'd make it." "Knowing" that you will make it one day is another very important part of the formula of success and will be covered later in this book.

5. Taking Advice from the Right People

The final characteristic I'd like to share about successful people is that they take advice from the right people.

What I mean here is: don't take advice or take things to heart said by those less successful than yourself, or those who have lower goals or ambitions than yourself. I know too many people who have come up with a great idea for a business or their dream life, get all excited about it, but when they tell their family and friends they say, "Is that really going to work?". Then the person thinks, "Perhaps they're right" and forgets the idea.

So, if you are looking for advice or inspiration, make sure it is from someone who's been there and done it and has goals and dreams as big as yours or bigger, otherwise they probably won't get it.

What often happens then is we look to defend our situation, because we want something different to our family and friends and very quickly they can feel we are saying they haven't been good enough or done enough with their lives. We need to avoid this. We need to avoid getting into a "who's right and who's wrong" argument.

It's not about right and wrong, it's just different. There are just different ways of thinking about life, the future, goals and security.

5

THE GOALS FORMULA

First of all, you need to think about your goals every day. Take New Year's resolutions. Many times I've heard people say in the middle of November that they have a fantastic idea, but then wait to set it up as a New Year's resolution. Then they do nothing for the next six weeks.

By the time these six weeks have passed, the passion might have died off or some doubts might have set in, and it'll never be set as a resolution.

If they'd started it, taken action and got on the way, they'd be six weeks further down the road – and they'd have avoided the risk of not starting it.

So, you need to sit and think about your goals every single day, where you want to be in life one year, three years, five years, ten years or more from now. What do you want your life to be like?

There is a proven formula for goals, which I will take you through, step-by-step, but first, here are the main stages in summary:

1. You've Got to Know What Your Goals Are

You've got to be able to set a goal statement so you know what you're going to do.

It's very important to have your goals written down. You need to write them down and carry them with you at all times, reading them on a daily basis.

I do. Every day I remind myself what my goals are and think about my future.

2. You've Got to Know You Deserve Your Goals – and That They Are Possible

This doesn't mean that you've got to believe it's possible for you at the moment. It means that it's possible in the world, as it were. If you can see somebody else doing it, then it's possible. The fact that you're saying it's not possible for you is probably some limiting belief or doubt, you just can't see a route to it. "How would I ever get into that circle of friends, that circle of people, how would that ever happen?" If you've got a goal you believe in, and you really believe you're going to get there to the point that you feel as if you've already achieved it, you're going to talk to people differently, you're going to behave differently, you're going to become a different person even before you get to the goal, and people are going to react to that because we all react to the people we come into contact with.

You've got to know your goal is possible and the rest will come when you've set your mind up correctly. Of course, you need to consider reasonable physical and other limitations. For example, if I set a goal that this time next year I would be able to flap my arms and fly at 10,000 feet off the ground (without any aids just my body) then that clearly isn't a realistic goal.

3. Act and Feel as if You've Already Achieved Your Goal

This is the most important one; and is the one that takes the work. Anyone who has watched the film *The Secret* or read the book will know that you need to think about your goal and what it will feel like when you've achieved it. They describe it from the viewpoint that, by doing this the universe will adjust itself and bring to you what you need.

On a personal level, I don't discount universal energies because I've had far too many things happen in my life to be coincidences or luck. However, I will explain this later in a way in which the logical and rational mind can appreciate and understand. You will be able to use this regardless of your personal beliefs about universal energies, simply by understanding how your brain is currently filtering information and how you can benefit from that knowledge.

4. Run a Daily Process of Thought Management

The fourth thing you have to do is what I call the "daily process of thought management". This gives you a structure in which to get the right feelings attached to your goal and set up in your mind a state of expectation for the day going the best that it could do, and as I have already said, our expectations influence our outcomes.

Now that you know the stages necessary for the goals formula I will take you through each step.

Knowing What Your Goals Are

Set a high enough goal that is compelling

Most of the time, we don't set a high enough goal for ourselves. We're afraid of how bad we'll feel if we don't meet it, and a lot of the time, if you don't set a high enough goal, you are unlikely to have big success ideas. There are a lot of things that won't even come into your awareness to do because you've not set the goal high enough.

For example, imagine you say to yourself, "This month I'm going to get two new customers," or you say, "This month I am going to get a hundred new customers." What do you need to do in either case?

You are quite likely to do very different things to get a hundred new customers compared to just two. There are going to be different strategies to making a plan to get at least a hundred new customers as opposed to just planning to get two. Getting just two more customers is a smaller goal, and so it's unlikely that you'll then stumble on big success. If you don't have big compelling goals, the big success ideas won't come to you. But what if you set a big goal for a hundred new customers and you "fail" because you only get fifty? How bad would that be? You've still got to set a high enough goal because you get different ideas at different levels, and you should never limit the possibility of exceeding your goals either. So in reality it would be best to set a goal for "at least" a hundred new customers in the above example.

You don't have to know how you will achieve it (yet)

The steps to achieving your goals will come. If you get that feeling of already achieved it, and how great it will be when you've achieved it, the steps you need to take to achieve the goal will become apparent to you. They will come into your awareness because you'll notice things in books you read, you'll notice things in what people say that you never picked up on before. We will explore this in detail in a later chapter.

When you set things up correctly in your mind, it changes your awareness and makes you act and behave differently – you'll be amazed once you get this working for you in your life.

If you start thinking and feeling what it would be like to achieve your goals, you will start to feel more enthusiastic. There will then be a slight difference in your tone – enthusiasm is in the tone – that will get picked up by other people. The actual words you use are likely to be different – more positive and more definite.

Language is so important, and the meaning is not so much in the words as it is in the tone. You can say, "Shut up!" in a joking tone, like a "that's not true you're just making it up" tone, or you can say "Shut up!" in an abrupt, commanding tone, for example, when telling someone off. These are the same words, but they convey a completely different meaning.

If you talk in a "down and dreary" tone to me, then my brain isn't going to feel very inspired, and I'm unlikely think about solutions for you. But if you're talking to me really enthusiastically about something, I'll think, "Well have you thought about this or have you spoken to this person?"

People will be different if you're different, and if you've got an air about you that you've already achieved it, and you know what it's going to feel like, your awareness will open up and these things will come to you.

It's not about "faking it until you make it". This is about being the person first on the inside before you become that person on the outside in the everyday world. Becoming the person on the inside first trains your brain for what you want to achieve, and then, once it's got the message, it will start to work out the way for you and bring appropriate opportunities into your awareness, as you'll see when we look at the "funnel of relevance" a little later.

What is your ultimate goal?

To make sure you've set yourself a really good goal, ask yourself this:

"If there was no risk of failure and money and education were not a problem, who would you be and what would you do?"

Do this exercise now – sit down for five minutes with a piece of paper and a pen, and write what your life would look like if you woke up on a Monday morning five years from now and everything in your life was perfect. What does your life look like?

Remember, this is a play pretend exercise, so you don't need to bring in any resistance or barriers such as "I'd never be able to achieve that."

Too many times I have met people who have heard me speak and want great success but fail to do this simple five minute exercise. Knowing isn't doing – the results come from doing not knowing! If you write continuously about your business life, home life, family, friends etc. – all aspects of your life – you end up with a page of goals!

Now you have this page of goals, this is what you need to think about often; and every time you think about them know how great it will feel when you are living that life.

But are your goals really your goals?

Thinking about your goals and dreams as described in the previous exercise does tend to alert your mind to what your ultimate goal might be, but the big question is of course:

"Is your ultimate goal really your ultimate goal?"

Sometimes people don't realize that when they say, **"My goal is I want to be a millionaire"**, the conscious mind loves that, it thinks about buying things and all the things that could mean. The subconscious mind, however, the powerful part of the mind, doesn't get engaged in it. It's only really interested, at a deep level, in your survival, if you don't need that to survive, it's not usually that interested, so it's an emotion that subconsciously may not get ranked very highly in the criteria order for most people.

If you've got a financial number in mind with one of your goals and you put your goal in those terms, ask yourself:

"What would that do for me?"
"What would that mean to my life?"

You may start coming up with things like, "Well, it would mean peace of mind, it would mean security, it would mean I'd be able to do things for others."

Now the subconscious mind loves these sorts of emotions, because it wants you to be safe. The subconscious mind thinks, "Peace of mind – that could lead to security. I love peace of mind and security. I'm the part that's responsible for your survival."

Whilst you don't necessarily need to have the peace of mind and security aspects in your goal statement, when you read the more materialistic description in your goal statement such as "be a millionaire", you need to be aware that these other things are behind it and linked to it.

You don't have to WANT your goal!

Wanting and Having Exercise

This exercise is most effective if you're sitting still and quiet in a room at home on your own. You may not get the whole impact if you're reading this in a noisy or disruptive environment, and because people experience emotions differently in different places.

I'd like you to think of a few things you really, really want – where you say to yourself "I want that"; you're really desperate for it.

Just write them on a piece of paper. Write: "I want" followed by what it is, just think of something that you really, really want, such as:

- I want a Ferrari.
- I want to own my own business.
- I want a fantastic relationship.

It could be anything that you want or are desperate for.

So, you have now written down these things you want.

The next thing is to write the same list out again, this time though starting each line with "I have". For example:

- I have a Ferrari.
- I have a successful business.
- I have a fantastic relationship.

Now you need to sit and read through, just in your head, your "I want" statements four or five times. Read them over and over and notice what sort of emotional tug you might get in response to them.

Then do it again, although this time with the second list of things, the ones starting with "I have". Notice what difference there is in the emotion response.

If I say to myself now, as I'm writing this, "I want", and then I say "I have", I can feel that difference on some level. It may be that I just know intuitively that it feels different or is different, but of course I'm used to noticing the link between words and attached feelings. I can very easily feel a noticeable difference – and many people can – but even if you can't at the moment it doesn't matter, it doesn't affect how well this can work for you.

If you read the two lists out loud as well, it will have even more impact, and very often the difference is easier to spot.

There is a small group of people who can really go after something and get it when they see something and say "I want that." For most people though, "wanting" is often a negative emotion.

Language is Important

When I got into personal development I realized that language was in many ways the most important part of it. The words we say to ourselves in our heads and the words we use with others are so important.

For most people, their brain sees wanting as a negative emotion because it can be associated with lack. It's something you haven't got, and not having it can make you unhappy or disappointed. The brain then wants to protect you, so it believes it's in your own interests to keep you away from the thing you "want" because you're saying "I want it". Wanting is often also associated with desperation and jealousy, which again are negative emotions. For most of us, when we were children and really wanted that special toy but our parents wouldn't get it for us, we felt desperate. We had no way, no resources to get what we wanted, and we knew there and then that wanting something really badly wasn't a good experience.

So the definition in your neurological system of wanting is likely to have some of those negative emotions attached to it. Your brain sees it as a negative emotion, so it doesn't think it's relevant to you even if you say "I want it, I want it."

However, when you say "I have it", the brain then thinks it's relevant, and it sets about identifying everything that brings that feeling about. This is the basis upon which the "already achieved it" feeling works as the most important component of goal-setting, which will be explored in detail a little later.

As I've said, the words you use are so important, and that's why we've got to avoid the word "want" when we talk about our goals. When we talk to others, we can say, "We're going to be . . ." and in our heads we've got to believe we're already there and feel what that's going to be like when we are actually there.

An important word you need to eliminate from your vocabulary as much as possible is "try".

Try isn't doing. If I say I'm going to pick a ball up, then obviously picking the ball up in my hand is "doing" it. "Trying" to pick the ball up can't be the same thing. It's got to be somewhere between picking it up and not picking it up. It's like intention without action.

Your motivation to do something is based upon how strongly you feel about it, and how compelled you feel to do it – feelings, that's what it's all about.

How compelled you feel to do something also depends on how you use the word try as well, but most of the time, trying isn't doing. Trying implies the possibility of not doing, so it's easier not to do it, and the reason we use the word try is because we don't want to be disappointed if we don't do it.

Most of the time the word "try" is used because you may not be fully committed to the action.

The trouble is, most of the time it's a killer because it means you're probably not going to do it, or you're not going to do it with as much enthusiasm.

We even do it to our friends. A friend phones up on a Friday morning and says:

"How about coming round? We'll have a few drinks later on, come round about 9 p.m.?"

You don't want to go and you say, "I'll try and come," because it's the easiest way out. You think you're being kind because you're letting them down gently, but, of course, they're not going to do anything else now because they think you might come round. However, it would have been better for them if you'd told them upfront, "I've got too much on. Sorry, but I can't come." At least they'd have known and they could have done something else, but instead our old villain the "try" word gets us off the hook if we don't do it or prevents us being disappointed if we don't achieve something. After all, we only said we would "try"!

You've got to say you're going to do it, whatever it is.

Because your goal is what you're going to become, you don't have to *want* it. As I said already, that's the wrong signal to send to the brain, you've got to get this "already achieved it" feeling – wanting is the wrong signal. Some people can get away with saying "want" and say, "I really want to be like them, I really want to do what they're doing", and go for it, as I said previously though, for most of us wanting isn't enough.

I didn't even know that I was going to end up getting into speaking and seminars. As I've told a number of people, probably about six years ago I was dead scared of getting on the stage and talking to anyone about anything, but when I sold my company I started to look at success and what had made me successful in many areas. I then applied what I had learnt to speaking in public and went from hating it to loving it! Until then it didn't enter my head to become a public speaker because I didn't like speaking at all. However, at one of the training sessions I attended with Paul McKenna, as I sat there in the audience and he was up there in front of a room of people I thought, "I could do that", and that's where it started.

When I said to myself "I could do that", I was in that environment, picturing myself up there talking to the people, and I was thinking that would feel fantastic, that would feel really good. I put myself in the environment to get the feelings and see what it would feel like.

That "already achieved it" feeling is what I was doing naturally. I had to break down and analyse where my success with the software company came from. When I was working in accounting, I was saying to myself, "It would be really great if I was working in computers", and I ended up working in computers, so then I said, "It would be really great if I owned my own software company", and then out of nowhere I set up my own software company. An opportunity I wouldn't otherwise have noticed came up, I didn't have to put a penny down, a company gave me money upfront to start my own computer software business and promised me another large payment when I delivered the software. The opportunity just appeared, and after two years I thought, "It would be really great if I could sell my business." I didn't know if I was going to be able to sell it, or to whom. I just thought, "It would be really great if I could sell my business." Then out of nowhere I sold my business to a Silicon Valley based US corporation at the time of the dot com crash. It was also just after September 11, 2001, so I sold it at one of the worst periods of uncertainty there was for the American economy in recent times. But it was those magic words I was saying to myself, "It will be really great if . . ." You have to find your own words, but for me, "It will be really great if . . ." actually makes my brain go out, see what that would feel like, and bring that future emotion back to me here and now.

Sometimes I would change it to, "It will be really great when . . ." For me that sounds more definite on a conscious level, when I think about it. However, in reality I've found ending in "when" or "if" still works for me, but again we're all different and you need come up with the wording or phrase that lets you experience how it will feel when you have achieved that goal and are living that life of your dreams.

Goal Statements

It's now time to look at some guidelines and rules about constructing your goal statement, a statement that leads to you experiencing that "already achieved it" feeling when you read it.

Hopefully you have already done the five minute exercise earlier in the book. If you had a page of many different goals then each of those individual goals could be used as a separate goal statement.

It's important to write your goals down and carry them around with you. A good tip is to carry your goal statements around on a small card and keep it somewhere you'll see it regularly – perhaps in a pocket, a wallet or purse. This will ensure you come across the card many times a day; and read your goal statements to develop a habit of thinking about your goals many times a day, feeling how good it will be when you've achieved those goals.

An interesting thing can happen in the development of habits. As you read that card more and more, very soon your brain will link your pocket, wallet or purse with your goal and its associated feelings. Then, whether you're aware of it consciously or not, every time you see your pocket, wallet or purse, or touch it, that goal statement is going to run in your head and reinforce it as part of you. This can then be generalized, and whenever you see any pocket, purse or wallet, or a picture of one, this goal statement can run inside your head, even outside of your conscious awareness. This happened to me with my own goal visualization about this very book. I attached my goal statement and how good it would feel so that it would run every time I saw a book – any book, anywhere!

Here are some guidelines for your goal statements:

1. Goals have to be stated in the positive

In life you notice and focus on what you think about most of the time. When you focus on a bad situation you are in, even if in doing so you wish things were different, then you attract more of that to you. This is simply because your brain is thinking about the bad situation and noticing things that relate to that bad situation.

If, instead of focusing on the bad situation you wish to get away from, you focus on the good situation you would like to experience, then things change. Now your brain will start to notice and focus on things that can lead you to the good situation you are looking for.

One of the biggest problems in personal development is when someone comes up to me and says, "Oh I wish my life were different."

I say, "Well what would you like to be different?"

They come up with statements like:

> "I don't want my personal relationships to be such a mess."
> "I don't want my business to be in ruin."
> "I don't want to be so poor."

Instead of telling me about the good situation they would love to have, they tell me about the bad situation they *don't* want! Focus on how you'd like things to be, as opposed to what you don't want:

> "I'd love to be in a fantastic relationship."
> "I'd like to own a successful business."
> "I'd love to have financial security."

Your brain is going to start thinking differently. Your brain looks to give you what you're searching for. If you start focusing on what you don't want, it's going to focus on that and think of things around that. It's highly unlikely that you're going to get many good ideas to point you in the right direction!

2. You need to make them personal

It needs to be obvious that this goal is about you. So start with or contain the word "I" so it relates to you, such as:

"I am going to . . ."

"I will . . ."

"I am . . ."

"I have . . ."

3. Use as few words as possible

It's really good if you can learn your goal statement off by heart so you can say it over and over in your head. It doesn't matter if it's a couple of sentences, but if it's a whole page, it's going to be harder for you to remember. Your brain is going to link that goal statement or phrase with the feeling you get when you constantly think about it and attach that feeling of what it will be like once that goal has been achieved. If you ended up with a whole page of notes from doing the exercise earlier about waking up five years from now, simply capture the highlights from that page to go on a summary list and they will remind you about the whole page whenever you read them.

4. Don't include "want"

Obviously, don't include the word want because, for most of us, the word want is too negative, as discussed earlier.

5. A definite timeframe

Your brain needs to have a definite timeframe in which the goal is to be achieved; you'll know what's realistic for you, and you'll have an idea of what's realistic and feasible in the world. People often say they don't know how long it will take, but if you think about it for a while, you probably have enough experience or common sense to have a pretty good idea.

If you're doing it financially, such as "I want to be worth £10,000,000 tomorrow", well, if you've got a big enough stake, and you've got the odds right, and you go over to Las Vegas, there might be a way of doing it. For most of us though, it's probably highly unfeasible that legally we could ramp up our financial situation to that degree in one day, especially if we're starting at or near zero.

If it was in five years time, that's probably far more feasible; so you need a timeframe. If you don't put a timeframe on it, the brain doesn't know how to prioritize. It makes decisions all the time about what to focus on and work out. Your brain could be thinking on a subconscious level:

> "All right I know it's relevant to them, I've got that, they've been to that event, they've been to that seminar, I've got the fact it's relevant, I can see that, but they haven't said when, so how do I prioritize? Perhaps it isn't that urgent and I don't need to give them a nudge about this opportunity I can see here."

So, you risk your brain seeing something that could lead to your success, and then it thinks, "I don't need to make them aware of that because they've got more important things to do today like watch something on the television."

You see, if someone who is starting at zero and their goal is to be a millionaire and they say they have no idea how long it will take, they are wrong. They probably have a pretty good idea.

I ask them, "Will it take a day?"

"No way more than a day," they reply.

"Will it take fifty years?"

"No, I think it could be done in way less."

Keeping moving the boundaries and eventually they end up with what they feel is a realistic timescale.

They had an idea of how long it would take all along but didn't think about it long enough to come up with an answer. They gave up too soon!

6. The goal must be in measurable terms

Goals must be set in measurable terms so you know and can test if you have achieved them, even if it's not a financial number. You've got to know what will need to be true in your life in order for you to know that you have achieved your goal.

How will you know when that goal is achieved?

However, you don't want that goal statement to be so specific it limits you:

As mentioned earlier you want to say "at least". "I'm going to get at least . . .", if there are some numbers in there, because what you don't want to happen, bizarre as this may sound, is to put off the chance of bringing into your awareness or going for opportunities that could take you much further than your initial goal just because you limited your goal statement.

Know You Deserve Your Goals and That They Are Possible

Overcome resistance to deserving your goal

You can add permission in the goal statement and say something like, "I allow myself to" or "I decide to" and then state your goal to ease the feeling if you sense some resistance or negativity towards it when you read it, such as you don't deserve success etc.

Some people talk about their goal and get quite a negative emotion about it for some reason or another. They may think that if they did achieve the goals they're setting it wouldn't be good for them – worrying what other people would think and things like that.

I had this when I first started setting my goals about speaking and about the personal development world. A problem I had was that I knew America was a really, really big market for me but, because I'd travelled so much in the past, my family wouldn't want me being away all the time. This was like a negative barrier to my goal-setting. However, I went with it and carried on thinking about it, believing a solution would come. Then I just had this idea that I could schedule anything I was doing in America during the school holidays, so we could take an extended family holiday. We could all go to America for, say, three or four weeks in the summer, and I could do a talk or a seminar once or twice a week perhaps.

I could have just shut that idea completely off so there was no point in even thinking about expanding the business into

America because I couldn't really go there as it was against the family values I had created for myself – but I didn't.

So, trust that a solution will come up, and sometimes when that solution comes up, it's obvious. You may even wonder why you didn't think of it before, but it's only when it's in your awareness. I let my brain know that I wasn't going to violate my values, and gave myself permission to still believe in that goal. The solution then came up, not immediately, but after a period of time of having belief and faith in my goal.

Example goal statements

So, here are some example goal statements:

This is a bad one:

> **"I want to write a book and become an author."**

It's got the word want in there. It's got a limitation because it just says "a book", i.e. no possibility of writing many books; also it has no timeframe in which it will be achieved. A better one might be:

> **"I will write at least two books and have them published in the next two years."**

Or another way of doing it is:

> **"It's 30 September 2014, and I've had at least two books published already."**

This last one is slightly better, but language is different for everyone. You've got to find a way of phrasing your goal statement so you can get that feeling of what it would be like that works best for you.

When I read the first one:

"I want to write a book and become an author."

It feels a bit flat to me, like, "Big deal, so what?"

When I say the second one:

"I will write at least two books and have them published in the next two years."

I start thinking about what that might be like. That's got a different feeling to it, and my brain is thinking, "Oh that's interesting," but when I say the third one:

"It's 30 September 2014, and I've had at least two books published already."

That feels more real, more definite, and it's easier to imagine being there and having achieved it.

So if you have already got a goal that you've been thinking about that might have been one of your "wants" initially, re-write it again following all these guidelines.

The goal statement you end up with is really the launch pad, which is why it's important that when you read it you get the correct feelings about achieving your goal. It fires off more detailed visualizations of what it will be like when it is achieved.

That "Already Achieved it" Feeling

Earlier I mentioned *The Secret*. If you are familiar with this film or book, you would have seen that it's about one main concept – if you want something in life you have just got to think about it, generate the feeling that you've already got it, and then it will manifest in your life. If you've got some doubt in there, it's not going to happen very easily.

The Secret describes how if you put the energy out there of feeling what it will be like when you have achieved your goal then the universe rearranges itself and brings you what you want. If we put the universe concept aside, there is another way of thinking about this. The whole principle of thinking and feeling what it will be like when your goal is achieved also affects how your mind works, what it focuses on and what it brings into your conscious awareness at any point in time, and, therefore, the opportunities you become aware of in any particular moment. Hence, regardless of your personal beliefs about the universe and manifesting you can see that the principle also applies to how your brain notices things and leads you to your goals.

This is how successful people, despite many failures along the way will very often say "I always knew one day I would make it".

In us, we've got the conscious and the subconscious parts of our mind. Now the subconscious can track millions of things at once, but the conscious mind can only track what we call "the rule of seven, plus or minus two things" at once. What that means is, it can track on average between five and nine things at the same time.

Therefore, the subconscious must act like a funnel and decide which five to nine things it's going to pass into your conscious awareness at a particular time. It decides that based on your beliefs, values etc. – and what it feels is relevant to you at that point in time.

So, one of the things probably not in your conscious awareness at the moment in your five to nine things is how your tongue feels in your mouth, but it probably is now! What has happened is that I have now made your tongue in your mouth "relevant". Your subconscious has dropped one of the things you were tracking on a conscious level and brought what your tongue feels like in your mouth into your conscious awareness. It's all based on what's relevant to you, what's going on in your life and the way you think about those things.

Now, going back to what I touched on earlier about the want emotion, the subconscious mind, for most people, sees wanting as a negative emotion. Therefore, the subconscious isn't really that interested in wants.

Here is an example of this, which I know many people have experienced. I wanted to get a black BMW, a specific model, and I told my friends that I'd show them the exact one I want as soon as we see one. We are out driving around in my current car, when all of a sudden coming down the road is the exact car I'm looking for. The subconscious notices it in all of the millions of things going on and has decided not to bring this into my conscious awareness. It knows that my association with the black BMW I really want is a wanting one and that is negative for me, so it doesn't distract my current thought trance or conversations, so I don't consciously notice it.

Eventually, of course, I purchase one I see advertised for sale, and again I may be out with friends, talking, listening to the radio, and again all of a sudden coming down the road is an identical one. This time, however, when my subconscious sees the car, it knows I now have an "already achieved it" or "I have" emotion associated with that particular object, so it knows it's highly relevant to me and should be one of the five to nine things I'm consciously aware of. This happens every time one comes along over the following days and weeks, and it seems to me that since I got one, loads more have appeared! They were always there; I just didn't notice them no matter how much I *wanted* to! There are no more or less than there ever were in reality, but my subconscious didn't class it as being "relevant" so I never noticed them previously.

The thing is, that car is just like a business opportunity, a step to your dream life. Many are probably passing you by each week because you aren't noticing them, because you haven't taught your brain that what you really want is relevant to you.

It also happens in relationships a lot. When you're not in a relationship, and you're out with your friends, you look and look and often can't meet anyone because you want to. However, quite often, as soon as you're in a relationship or get married, it can seem like everyone is interested in you – opportunities seem to be everywhere! Why? We notice more people interested in us than before and often think, "Where were they all when I was single these past months?" The fact is, with respect to the relationship, you now have "an already got it" emotional attachment, so you act different, look different and notice different things.

So, practice and start to feel what it's going to feel like when you're there, what it will be like, not "I really want to be doing that" or "I really want that to happen". If your goal is to own a big house, then go and view a big house and walk around one. You'll have a better mental image to build on, and when walking around it, you'll be able to play pretend and imagine what it would feel like to be living in such a house.

The mind is an amazing thing. It's like when I was thinking I wanted to start a new business, but I didn't really know what in. I used to walk down the same street passing the same billboard every day but didn't notice it. As soon as I attached this meaning of, "I've already started my business and I can see myself being really successful", all of a sudden the billboard was drawn to my attention. On that billboard was something that gave me an idea about the business. If you can attach the emotion of what it's going to be like when you've already got it, you'll start to find that things come into your awareness that your brain automatically ignored previously.

There is this subconscious processing going on that is deciding what you notice and don't notice. No matter how hard you think consciously, or look for something, unless big brother – the subconscious – decides that it's relevant, you're going to have to practically fall over it.

So, the above then is a more logical explanation of how attaching feelings of having "already got it" works to manifest what you truly desire in your life. What you are doing is playing a trick on the brain and making it believe you already have what you want. This then leads you to notice the opportunities that will lead you there. You are simply using the natural "relevance matching" function of the brain to achieve your goals.

When I started to look at and analyse all the things I'd done in my life, I remembered when I was about fourteen and watching television programmes like *Dallas* and *Dynasty*. I never used to think, "Oh, lucky rich . . ." and all that sort of negativity like my friends at school. As you now know, to feel jealousy associated with something you want would be negative. I remember I thought it would be really cool to own my own business and drive around in nice cars. I used to think that would be really great. I applied the "already got it" emotion, thinking how I'd feel if I was in that situation.

Take celebrities. You often hear people say they hate certain celebrities, but most of the time they don't actually hate them, they're simply jealous of their wealth and their success because it reminds them of what they haven't achieved themselves.

For example, if you're a shy, quiet person at a party, you would probably hate the noisy, rowdy people, but would actually love to be more like them. Quite often, you don't like things in others that will remind you of a limitation in yourself.

The problem with being envious or jealous when you see those with things you'd like is that you're wasting all the work you put into the "already achieved it" feelings and thoughts. As soon as you get jealous or envious of those with the things you'd like, you're telling the brain it's bad, wrong and, therefore, not right for you.

When I see someone with the life I'd love to have or the possessions I'd like, I say to myself, "Wow how cool it would be to have that?" You have to find the words that work for you in this situation, but again, I'm constantly programming myself so my mind knows what I'm to become or have in my life.

These things are possible when you get into that positive "secret to life" zone where everything works out well.

You're not going to necessarily believe in it on day one, and that's why if you do the daily process, which we'll look at later, you'll get more used to this feeling of already having it and you'll think about your goals straight after that. Your brain will get more used to putting that goal statement with that "already got it feeling" emotion, and then you'll notice different things happening and coming into your awareness, some of them really freaky as well. You may start to pass these off as coincidences, but then there'll be far too many just to be coincidences.

The best way I know of getting that "already achieved it" feeling is to have a really good vision in your mind of what it's going to be like. This inspires you to get that feeling when you're saying, "Wow, that's going to feel fantastic, it's going to be brilliant when I'm doing all that, it's going to be really, really cool."

So, you've got to think about your goal and see yourself already having that, feeling what it feels like, thinking about how you'd walk, how you'd act, how you'd talk, how others would see you, what you'd be like as that person who you'd be when you achieve that goal.

The brain, that small, childlike bit in there, the inner child, that's still governing most of what we're doing, loves playing pretend, and it can really attach great emotions to it. Now initially you may not get very strong emotions, but later when we go through the daily process, you'll start to see that it's structured in such a way that you get used to feeling that "already achieved it" emotion ready for when you think about your goal, so you can start to transfer these emotions over.

When I thought about writing this very book, I thought, "I'm going to write a book and get it published by a mainstream publisher, and what will that be like? What will it feel like? How will I act? What will I do?" I made this picture in my head that I'd go into this large bookshop in London on Charing Cross Road. I go in, up an escalator, and when I get up to the top, all the personal development books are there, including mine. So, whenever I think about what it would be like if I wrote my own book and got it published, I see myself going into that bookstore, I see myself going in the doors, I see myself walking over, going up the escalator, look over to the personal development books, and I can see my book on the shelf, and I notice as I get closer that there's somebody looking at my book, browsing through it. I go over and I say to them, "You know the author's in the store today if you wanted to get that signed."

They turn round and say, "Is he?"

I tell them to turn to the back cover. They turn to the back cover and there's this moment of realization when they realize it's me in the author's picture, and I turn to them and say, "I'll sign it for you now if you like!"

Now that sounds bigheaded perhaps, but that's what the brain loves, that sort of situation where you take your goal, and you embed it in what could happen in an everyday occurrence because it thinks, "Wow, that would be really cool, that would feel really, really great."

So, with that sort of visualization in my mind, and the feelings it generates, how easy do you think it would be to get on and write the book instead of thinking about the hours slaving over a keyboard wondering what to write next? All I did if I slowed down was to run that scene in my head again and realize, "Yes, that's why I'm doing it," and I got back to the writing.

Now every time I see a book, someone reading a book or writing in a book, it makes me smile inside and I feel good. No doubt my brain is running in the subconscious this little movie, making me feel good thinking about books.

Think back to when you were a child. You'd play pretend, believing it was reality. Your brain loved it. It was only when adults came along and told you to stop being stupid and mucking about that you stopped doing it, but that part of the brain is the powerful part. What I'm asking you to do, nobody else can see, nobody else knows about, it doesn't cost you a penny to do and it doesn't take any time. You can run your goal visualization while you're waiting for a bus, while you're sitting on a bus, while you're sitting in the car at traffic lights or while you're walking down the street. You can incorporate it into everyday activities, and in those times your brain would normally run around thinking about useless negative things.

You imagine being in that situation, and if you really think about it, there's some amazing little movies you can play in your head of what it will be like when you've got your ultimate goal or you've achieved that particular goal – you could be setting multiple goals at the same time of course.

A "touch it" approach and vision boards

An alternative approach if you find visualization tricky is to take a "touch it" approach.

Say your goal is to have a really big house. Go and view the sort of house you want because then in your mind you're going to make a much better mental image of what that's going to be like to help in your visualization and what it's going to feel like.

For example, it feels really good when you go round there thinking, "This is where I'm going to have breakfast, that's where we'll have the library, that's where we'll do this, that's where we'll sit of an evening and listen to music, that's where we'll keep the horses . . ." – if that's your thing.

You can build all that in your mind while you go round viewing the house if your visualization skills aren't getting you there. That's what I call the "touch it" approach, or, of course, there are vision boards.

People use vision boards and swear by them. You've probably seen this, they get a picture of their ideal house or the ideal place they want to live, or whatever, and they put it on the wall. They look at it every day, and they see it every day, then that manifests for them. It all leads to connections to your "already achieved it" emotional attachment going on.

If you've got the picture of the ideal house or the ideal life-style on the wall, and you look at that and you think, "Wow that's going to be so fantastic", and get the "already achieved it" feeling, you're programming it into your mind.

After a while, you won't look at it every day, or you won't notice it, you'll walk past it, but the thing is, it's like what happens at home when you rearrange the room, it feels fantastic and you think, "Why didn't we do this before? This feels like a brilliant room now, it feels totally different." After a few weeks, you get used to it and you don't notice it anymore. Now that happens with the vision board, but, of course, the subconscious mind notices it all the time, it keeps noticing it. Every time you go past it, you may not be paying attention to it, but it's getting logged time and time again.

So some people like the vision board approach and find it works well for them. I know loads of people who do use them, and it can greatly help visualization if visualization is an issue for you.

Remember when you do all this and start getting little feelings that perhaps you should take some particular action or talk to someone – you must do it! These are signs from your intuition and subconscious that are there for a reason, do not miss the opportunity to take any action that could well be vital to you achieving your dream life.

The Daily Process of Thought Management

When you know what your goal is, you know you deserve it, and that you've got to attach the "already achieved it" feeling to it, then it's time to set up your all-round personal development daily process. This does not just have to be for goals, it can be used for day to day life as well.

This is something you could be doing every day. Here are the steps:

What's right in my world?

First thing in the morning, when you wake up, you need to think about what's right in your world. Make a list of all the things that are right in your world that you like, that you love, that you're grateful for, and read that list every morning. This gets your mind in a positive mindset as soon as you get out of bed. If you don't get into a positive state, it's likely you'll get into a negative mindset. This is just the way the human brain and the body are built for most people; it's likely to go negative unless you get it positive.

So, when you get up, you will start thinking about all that's right. This might be things you're looking forward to such as a holiday, or things you're doing that day, or what you did last week with family, friends, children . . . whatever, job, anything that makes you feel good. Maybe it's even the fact that you're grateful for your health, and that you've woken up that day.

Think about your goal as much as possible through the day and feel as if it's already happened

All the items you went through in step one of the daily process are things you have and are grateful for, and, therefore, the feelings you get when thinking about them are like an "already achieved it" feeling. Having just experienced the feeling of thinking about what you have and are grateful for, you can now easily know when you have the same or similar emotion attached to your goals.

There are loads of things that can remind you of your goals. You'll see something and think: "That's what I really want", so run that goal vision with that "already achieved it" feeling. See yourself in the situation that the other person is in, like me seeing Paul McKenna on the stage. Every time you come across your goal card in your wallet, purse, pocket, or wherever you keep it, think about it, read it a number of times, relax and feel how great it feels to achieve that goal and have all that the goal brings into your life.

Plan your day and see it going the best it can

Now this is very powerful and important. In the mornings, you want to plan your day, see it going the best it can go, think about all those meetings and appointments you've got coming up, and rather than start thinking about what might go wrong, see them go the best they can go.

Do this in the morning, and then before each activity, before you go into a meeting, run it again and see it going the best it can. You're going to go in with more enthusiasm, and you're going to go in with the expectation of a good result.

Now a lot of people dismiss this stuff, but what's going to make you feel better – thinking about going in there and it all going fantastically, or thinking it's a waste of time and it's all going to go badly?

If you think about something going badly before the event you're going to come across completely differently, even if you put a brave face on as soon as the door opens. You've got to have this expectation of a good outcome. It's not guaranteed, but it's an expectation, because what that does guarantee is that more often than not it will go right for you. You see it going the best way it can and this is so powerful – and also very, very important.

End of day review and fix

Every night when I get into bed and I turn the light off, and I lie down and do this step. It sounds weird, but this is amazing as well.

Review what happened during the day including the things that didn't go as well as they could have gone. Imagine them going better, so even if it was somebody who said, "No, we're not interested", imagine they said, "Yes, great, fantastic", or them saying they'd give you a call in a few weeks.

Imagine it, and fix it, if you made a mistake. For example if you had a meeting and you said something really bad, imagine the meeting without you saying it, and when you do that, you want to repeat the process five or six times. Say it over and over five or six times, because you'll be surprised that the emotion attached to that event will very likely be different then and, of course, that's going to impact the next day and how you approach it.

When you start the next day, if you've still got that bad emotion about that last call or the meeting that went badly, that will affect the first call or the first meeting of the next day, to some degree.

It's not what happens, it's the meaning and, therefore, the emotion you attach to it.

So what's the problem if you just cheat it a little bit? You've "already achieved it", that's a trick on the brain, but you're using its mechanisms to slightly fool it so that you get to where you really *want* to be in life. I use this method a lot.

You can still feel a bit negative, a bit down about it, but it changes it to a degree. Sometimes, for me, it completely eliminates it so that the next day I don't even think about it. Often it's reduced it and made it a lot better.

You can do that at night and also right after the event. The important thing here is what you "could" have done not "should" have done.

"Should" is often a bad word, as it focuses you on what went wrong. "Should" for most people has an element of guilt attached too. So don't use "should", use "could".

What you *could* have done empowers you to think about doing it again in a different way – it focuses you. If you say, "I should have said this, I should have done that, and I should have said the other, that's why I didn't get the deal", it's not empowering you much for the future. If you change the tone to be upbeat and encouraging and the words to, "I could have done this, I could have said that, I could have said the other", that's building pictures in your mind of you doing it again in the future in a better, more empowered way, and you're thinking more about what you're going to do next time than what you did last time when you got what was really only an unplanned outcome. You probably thought it was a failure before you read this book!

6

A BRIEF RECAP ON GOALS

So, a brief recap on Part One then.

Constant repetition is the key. You need to get this goal visualization ingrained in your mind, thinking about the goal as "already achieved it" – it needs to become a habit.

You've got to think about it every day, and you've got to find things in the environment that you see every day that will inspire you to think about your goal and remember it. Remember it from this "already achieved it", already got it state and you will start to notice the little prods inside you. You've got to act on these little prods that tell you that you ought to just talk to that person, you ought to just make that call, or you ought to just go to that event.

You have to act on those inner nudges or feelings that you ought to do something rather than say, "Oh no, it's not me", because we don't realize what the consequence of that statement or avoiding action might be.

So many times I've gone with things even though they felt uncomfortable only to have some fantastic outcome, and then worry afterwards "What if I hadn't taken action, I'd never have got this outcome!"

I heard something recently, I'm sure it wouldn't happen to anybody reading this, but someone had been invited on a couple of occasions to appear on radio and turned it down because "It might be awkward, might feel awkward", but what an opportunity! We need to take the opportunities when they're out there, we need to go and say, "Well, maybe, but that's part of my goal, this could be my goal, this could be a prod, this could be it."

We don't know how many prods we're going to get, so we need to pay attention, and some things might be uncomfortable – true, they could be – but if your goals are clear, you can use that to motivate you through.

So, you've got to have enthusiasm, you've got to have expectation and that feeling of "already achieved it", that's the real key.

Of course, even with the "already achieved it" feeling, you can still come up against things you need to do that, for some reason or another, are very uncomfortable due to fears and phobias. This is what we're now going to look at in Part Two – Being the Best You That You Can be, How to Remove the Barriers to Your Goals and What You Want to Achieve in Life.

Part Two

BEING THE BEST YOU THAT YOU CAN BE

7

HOW YOUR BRAIN MANAGES EXPERIENCES

As mentioned in Part One, the brain has a conscious part that controls your logical reasoning, your current thinking and your awareness – your five to nine things going on at once. This is also the part where you start thinking it would be really great to do something.

The other part, the subconscious, is absolutely amazing, you don't have to think about breathing, you don't have to think about pumping the blood round your body or your heart beating, this is all taken care of every second of every day.

Unfortunately, there are a lot of other things the subconscious does automatically without you having to really think about it – like playing back your fears and phobias automatically. It tells you that you can't do something for example in a particular situation, giving you that fear or negative emotion.

I always think of the subconscious as a Sky+ machine, which allows you to pause, record and rewind the TV.

So, why do I think of the Sky+ machine being like the subconscious? At an early age, if something happens that has a degree of emotion attached to it, the brain stores what happened away like a little movie and can play it back for you whenever it feels you are in a similar situation. It gives you the same emotion now that you felt when the original experience happened.

In fact, everything you do has an emotion attached to it. So, for instance, if somebody, a family member or anyone, put a spider on you to scare you when you were young, you're likely to get a bad emotion attached every time you see a spider later in life.

Your brain wants to help by putting as much as possible on autopilot. It spots a problem and puts it on autopilot for you, so you won't ever have to decide about being scared of that particular thing again. This is good for some things, but it isn't good for others. So, every time that person sees a spider, they get the emotion and panic related to the original event, which is stored in the Sky+ memory of the brain.

To the onlooker, it seems like the panic is instant when the person sees the spider. There is, however, a very small window – milliseconds – between when they see that spider and then panic. In that small window of time, they run a little program, what we call their strategy, the way they react and then behave in a given circumstance. This is their strategy for dealing with spiders, so they may run a little movie in their head, which they may or may not be consciously aware of. They might see a spider run towards them and run up their leg, or hear someone scream or panic and then that gives them their strategy, that's how they deal with "spiders", so it just replays itself.

When you start to look at things, this autopilot can be very useful. A good example is driving. When you start to learn to drive, it's all in the conscious mind. When I started to learn to cope with the many things like the mirrors, the clutch, the gear stick, the indicators, the steering wheel – all these things you've got to do, all these multiple things – I sat there sweating and thinking on my first, second and third driving lessons that I was never going to be able to do this. Then one day it clicks, and all of a sudden you're driving, and you get home thinking, "Did I look at the traffic lights, were they red, I didn't look at that roundabout did I?" You see, the autopilot has taken over, it's said, "I've got this driving game down now, so you don't have to worry about it, you find something else for your five to nine things to pay attention to in your conscious awareness, because I'm taking care of driving in the subconscious."

How You See the World

The other thing the subconscious does for us is control where our comfort zone is, when our fight and flight responses come in, and our beliefs, our values, our limiting beliefs and our empowering beliefs. Our values are things like honesty and integrity, love and connection, safety and security. It also controls our strategies. We're going to explore strategies shortly, as well as the little movies or programs that play on autopilot, like the spider and driving examples, and not forgetting of course our "map of the world".

We've all got a "map of the world", which is what the world means to us and how we see ourselves in the world, and they're all slightly different. Some are also a lot different to our own. This is why two people can go to the same event and have a completely different perspective on it. Two friends can go to the same function, for example, and, coming out, one might say, "Weren't all the people friendly?" and the other, "No, all the people were horrible and miserable."

What happens very often in life is that we self-manifest our reality because so much comes across in our body language, which is generated at a subconscious level. A person who is shy will go into the room thinking no one is going to talk to them, they'll be looking down, they'll stand over in the corner, and everyone else will be thinking things like, "Well, they don't want to be disturbed, they've obviously got something on their mind, better leave them alone."

If another person, a confident one, comes in, they see the whole room, just make eye contact and connect with people, even at a distance, and create their own reality. So, you see, it's all about how you go into situations, what's going through your mind, and we're going to explore this later, especially when it comes to going to events, meetings and other situations, and how you set that up in your head beforehand.

Your expectations have a massive impact on how well things go. This is true for whatever it is you're going into because people will react within a few seconds of you going into a room. You don't have to say anything, they're reacting from this prehistoric part of the brain that's actually unknown to us, you may have noticed for instance when you stand in a supermarket queue, somebody stands behind you and you get a funny feeling about them. You don't know quite what it is, but you've just got a funny feeling about them. This is all part of subconscious communication.

It's like earlier, when I was saying about things we say to ourselves in our heads. You may say things like, "I'm in two minds about what to do." That's bizarre, in two minds. "You know, part of me wants to, part of me doesn't." You probably say things like this all the time, and the language you use is generated subconsciously.

Normally, when you're talking and having a conversation or saying things, words are coming out subconsciously based on the emotional attachment to experiences. When you're in the flow, you don't consciously think of the next word that's coming out of your mouth. It just flows, it just comes out, and it's all built or constructed automatically. You can get a good idea about someone's beliefs in what they say, and you can even tell what's having more impact on them, whether it's the pictures they're making in their mind or whether it's the things they're saying to themselves when they're talking to themselves in their head or when they're talking to you because they'll tell you with the language or words they use.

So, your "map of the world", or the way you see the world and your part in it, can be very different to someone else's, and that's why you will experience things differently. You simply see the world differently to other people. You also have a sense or belief about how you are perceived by others in the world. Everyone has their own unique map.

8

STRATEGIES (OR THE WAY WE THINK ABOUT THINGS)

When an event happens, you first sense it through one or more of the five senses, whether that's things you see, hear, smell, taste or touch. That sense goes into your brain. Then comes the emotional feeling that causes you to decide what that event means to you and how you react to it. Notice I said what the event means *to you* and not what the event just means!

Very often at the end of a talk or presentation I will ask the audience if there are any questions on what I have spoken about. Usually this results in a deadly silence. I then explain to the audience that I could take the fact there are no questions to mean that the audience didn't like the talk and, therefore, don't want to engage with me and cannot wait to get away. Or I could take the silence to mean I have done such a good job of explaining things that no-one even has any unanswered questions about what I have been teaching them. Which "meaning" I select not only says a lot about my own beliefs but also has a great bearing on how I feel in that moment and whether I am likely to do another talk again or not!

Think about this situation – you are walking towards your place of work and you see a client coming towards you, you smile and say hello, but they ignore you. Do you think they don't like you or were pretending to not see you? Or do you assume they didn't recognize you or hear you? Perhaps they have just had some bad news and their mind is elsewhere.

Here is how we manage our daily experiences, an external event happens, we see a spider or think about making a cold call on the phone, then we process the information or event based on:

- our beliefs and values;
- our experiences to date;
- our assumptions about the future; and
- our "map of the world".

All of this creates what we call our internal representation, i.e. how we represent (or "re-present") to ourselves the actual event inside our minds.

You have to visualize everything before you do it, which of course happens really quickly, and you don't always notice it on a conscious level. For instance, if you drive, the only way you are going to find your way back to your car is by picturing where it is, and you have to do that, you don't just *know* where it is.

A lot of people don't believe that initially, it takes practise sometimes to notice what images are coming into your mind, and the things you say in your head just before you get that emotional feeling determine what action, if any, you take.

Your internal representation then controls your thoughts, and as we know from earlier, your thoughts create your emotional state, your quality of action and your outcome and results. These thoughts are a cluster of things called "thought strategies".

A strategy is a cluster of thoughts made up of pictures we imagine or remember, things people have said or we say to ourselves, feelings we get or remember, smells we remember or sense, and even taste memories. Some of this can be out of conscious awareness as it runs very quickly in your mind. However, you need to slow it down so you can start to notice these things going on in your mind. The one thing I really hope you get out of this is that once you've opened up awareness to how this works and I've pointed some of these tools and ideas out to you, you will start noticing more, especially when you get a bad emotion or feeling in a certain situation.

The next time you notice yourself overcome with a feeling of negativity ask yourself what were you thinking to cause yourself to feel like this? The more you do it, the more you practice and the more you can then start to trap what's going on. You can then start to realize the pictures you're making and the things you're saying to yourself. You can start to slow it down and realize what's going on inside your head. It might even be a memory of a teacher saying, "Oh you'll never amount to much", and things like that. And it's rather common that parents or teachers quite unknowingly have embedded something in your head.

Actually, one of the more recent discoveries is that, apparently, when people come around after having have had an operation, and they've been unconscious, under hypnosis, they can then relay every single word that the surgeon said while they were in the operating theatre. So, when the surgeon said something like, "I can't see him lasting six months after this, we've done the best we can", that's now planted in that person's subconscious mind, and that sets them up for how they're going to go forward. So you've got to be so careful with language and what you say to yourself and to others.

What happens, then, is we make pictures and movies in our heads when we imagine or think about something. If we think about something we're going to do and say something to ourselves or remember something someone else said, or a smell or a taste, then one or more of these internal senses can loop around, and we call this collection of internal representations your "strategy".

A real popular one for smells firing emotions off is when adults go into a school building, and they get that feeling of when they were at school. Often it's the smell of the floor polish that sets that off with a lot of people, although they don't realize it. Out of all the senses, smell goes straight to the emotional part of the brain and generates the emotion. It's the fastest sense for generating emotion because it doesn't go through any other filters. Everything else goes through belief filters and other mechanisms before the resulting emotion, but smell doesn't.

Now, one or more of these internal representations will loop and follow a sequence, so with the spider phobia, it might be:

See a spider (the external event)

Their strategy then might be to:

Make a picture in their mind or recall a picture of a hairy spider running towards them

And then:

Hear their mum say, "Oh god! It's a spider!"

And then:

Get a bad feeling

And then:

Panic and run out of the room screaming!

That's their strategy.

Now, someone else's strategy for dealing with that same external event might be totally different, they might:

See a spider (external event)

And then:

Say to themselves, "Oh look, it's a spider. I'd better not tread on it."

And then:

Pick the spider up in a glass and put it in a safe place outside!

That probably sounds bizarre to someone who's got a spider phobia, but that's a lot of peoples' strategy to some degree or another. These are totally different outcomes to the same event based on *how* the people concerned are thinking about it or their strategy for dealing with a spider.

Your strategy in a given context is how you do what you do.

You can sit down and analyse your strategy as to why, for example, you don't want to call someone. Perhaps it's because you think you might interrupt them, or they might not want to hear from you. You might think you could be being a nuisance, perhaps you're picturing them on the other end of the phone thinking, "S/he's a nuisance". But whatever your strategy is, that's the reason why you're not making the phone call, how you are thinking about it. You make a picture, you say something, you make another picture, then you get the feelings, and that's what we call the structure of your strategy, that's your sequencing. This order of feelings, pictures, sounds etc. is just an example, we are all different and structure the order of these elements and which elements are included based on the way we as individuals process information, and it can vary from situation to situation.

This example is in the context of making a phone call, but it isn't the same sequence for another fear you may have such as a fear of giving a presentation or a fear of doing something else. The strategies can be different, the structures can be different, so, unfortunately, you don't get the structure and answer to everything, but what you do get is your strategy in a given context or aspect of your life which tells you how you do what you do. Of course, you also have empowering strategies that really help you perform to the best of your current abilities in various situations. Notice I said your *current* abilities – this says you can or could improve your abilities in the future. If I had just said best of your abilities it would imply you could never improve or change, this is why language and the words we use are so important. They are making impressions on our mind that we are creating feelings about and storing away as experiences to affect us on another occasion.

How effective we are at anything we do is based on the strategy we run just beforehand, so if you interfere with someone's strategy that's how you can mess them up.

A tightrope walker who never used a net was in the news a few years back. Throughout his entire previous tightrope walks, he never fell. Then he went to a venue where the health and safety people said he had to have a net, and he fell because the net was there! Previously he probably just saw himself glide across to the other side but this issue about having a net and seeing it there likely caused him to start thinking about falling and imagine what it would be like to fall!

So, your strategy in a given context is how you do what you do.

Here are two everyday strategies I like to talk about to help people understand and notice exactly what their own strategies are.

I recall Richard Bandler explaining this first one in a training session I attended a number of years ago when I was looking to understand how I had achieved the success I had. In a restaurant, we've all got a strategy to decide what we want from a menu. This is even more complex when we go out with a group of friends because we all sit there around the table, we get our menu and, depending on our strategy, decide what we want to eat.

My wife's strategy is to check out the desserts first; then she will go down the list of main courses. When she gets into the dessert category, she might just go in sequence, or she might scan for something and she might just read the first line of each menu item, such as chocolate gateaux, and then she might make a picture of it in her mind of what it might look like and think, "Oh go on then."

We all have a strategy, a way of doing this. Other people might start by choosing a starter, and then choose a main course. It's very complex to actually get to that decision, you have to go through all that processing because some people, like me for example with the mains courses, go through the list first and say no to all the fish items and then say no to all the meals that might actually look like an animal! Then when I start to go through the potentials, like fillet steak, I'll imagine a picture of the steak and think what that's going to look like, and what that's going to taste like. I do that and carry on until I make a decision.

What happens is that moment comes, especially if you're the first, when you say, "I know what I'm having." You then turn to the person next to you and say, "What are you going to have?"

They reply, "I'm having the fish."

"Oh, I was going to have the fish," you say. Then you've got to go all back through it again because you don't want to *not* have it, and they have it, and it is nice, but if you change, you're going to have to re-evaluate everything again, not just the main courses, but potentially the starters and desserts, because they may not go with the new main course!

That's why I said it's a really complex strategy. Next time you're sitting down looking at a menu deciding what you're going to have, just say to yourself, "How am I deciding?" Are you picturing things? Are you saying something in your head? Are you imagining what each item will taste like?

Now that I've mentioned this, you'll become more and more aware of the things that normally happen on autopilot and are normally out of your conscious awareness, happening so fast you don't realize you are doing it most of the time.

It's like the person with a spider phobia, a lot of the time they see the spider and just panic. They don't think about the little strategy running inside their heads where they're creating their own panic on a subconscious level.

In life, we often rush around here there and everywhere, and people say you've got to slow down, but you haven't got to slow down, you've got to calm down! That's what you've got to do because when you're not calm, that's when your fight or flight mechanism from the subconscious mind kicks in. You get all emotional, start generating panic, stress or fear emotions and the brain wants to protect you and preserve its power for your survival in the pending flight or fight situation it believes you are about to face.

When you're not calm, it cuts off a lot of your potential. As soon as you get yourself in a bit of a state, you can't think straight, and you can't see what to do next. All these signals tell you that you've got yourself into this confusion and you need to calm down. Only when you are calm and composed will you be able to maximize your potential, your skills and your knowledge of dealing with things. It's like when you can't remember someone's name. No matter how frustrated you get the answer doesn't come until you put it aside, calm down and get on with something else – when you are calm the answer comes.

So, back to strategies . . .

Walking. This is a classic; walking. You know when you're in a crowded street; some people have got a really good walking strategy. You've seen them, they just walk straight through and it's like the parting of the Red Sea. Everyone gets out of their way; they just cruise through, just walk! Whereas other people just bump into everyone, and they get into that "you go, no you go" dance, where they end up going in the same direction when trying to avoid each other. What happens then is that both people have got the same strategy where if they come in front of somebody like that, they move aside. This can happen several times and end up like a dance because the two keep running and re-running the same strategy to move aside.

There is always that one person who bumps into everyone and has basically got a bad strategy.

They are probably walking along saying something to them-selves in their head like, "I mustn't bump into people", or perhaps they are saying to themselves something like, "There's a lot of people, I've got to avoid other people." But their focus is on the people, and like the tightrope walker falling off the rope, no matter how hard you try, you're going to be drawn towards the people as you walk, if you're thinking about "avoiding the people".

The people who walk in busy places and just cruise along probably have a good strategy where they focus on the gaps and space around the people, rather than the people themselves. When they focus on a gap, no matter how small, and head towards that gap, then most of the time the people coming the other way will have moved slightly to enable them to pass through the gap.

In life, you must remember that you mustn't think about what you don't want; you've got to think about **what you'd like things to be like or what you are looking for**.

If you think about what you don't want, you actually get attracted to what you don't want. If you say to someone "don't be scared", they start thinking about being scared; it would be better to tell them to be calm, you've got to think about the outcome.

The outcome that you want is what you've got to focus on.

Developing a New Strategy

There is research that says to develop a habit you have to do something for over twenty-eight to thirty-two days consecutively and then you'll implant a habit. If you're learning a new skill or doing something different like playing tennis for example, then, on average, you have to do it about fifty times to gain a reasonable level of competence so you can play at a good level.

The average adult gives up in less than ten attempts when doing something new; and that's a large part of the problem. As adults, we won't do the child strategy of looking at the results we're getting, adjusting our approach, seeing if that improves our results or makes our results worse, and adjusting accordingly, as a continual check, adjust, check, adjust to get to where we want to be. That's what Edison did with the light bulb; he had 10,000 attempts, or something like that, before he finally got the light bulb to work and people used to say to him, "Doesn't it bother you that you failed 10,000 times to get a light bulb to work?"

He said, "I haven't failed 10,000, times, I've discovered 10,000 ways to not make a light bulb work and I'm getting closer." All the time it's getting closer, this belief that he's getting closer. Of course, this Edison story appears in many variations over the years of 1,000 times, 5,000 times and 10,000 times, but the fact of the matter is the principle is one of the fundamental aspects of success and learning.

Here's a little exercise, you can do it in your head, it's quite easy:

What colour is your front door?

If you think about what colour your front door is, the only way you can answer that is to make a picture of it in your mind. Now if you think you aren't making a picture of it, it's only because the picture is running too fast and you aren't yet consciously aware of it.

So a good question to help you slow the picture down so you can notice it is this:

How does the door open, does it open to the left or the right?

To answer that question, you've got to hold a picture in your mind longer to answer and you get more of a chance of seeing it!

Some people visualize really, really well. What they'll do is use their hands to work out which way the door opens by imagining they were actually opening the door. I always remember this specific example of which way the door opens. I was in full flow speaking at a conference and had just asked the audience to think about their own door and if it opened to the left or the right, so they could notice a picture of the door in their minds. A hand went up in the audience and I asked the man what he wanted, he said, "Am I standing inside or outside the house?" Sometimes you can't predict what someone will throw at you. Of course it didn't matter, the answer wasn't important; it was noticing the process or the pictures that came to mind that was important.

These pictures are in our minds, but to get perspective and organize the images our brains actually project them forwards so we can get a sense of where the picture seems to be. For example, it could be straight in front, off to the left, the right or anywhere.

It's like when somebody says they went on holiday and they went out and had this fantastic meal. They make some gesture with their hands as to the size of the meal. What they're doing at that point is telling you they are picturing that meal and they've got really good association at the moment with this space; we call it a spatial anchor. They have created a spatial anchor of something they really liked or felt good about.

We all place images out there in our perspective space.

If I were to ask you to think of someone you like and picture them, then think of someone you don't like and picture them, there'll be something different about the structure of the pictures.

Your brain doesn't really know if you like them or not based on just the content; the way it knows is by the way it stores the pictures, which in turn is based on the feelings or emotions you felt when the image was stored.

It's a bit outside the scope of this book, but some people might place people they like on the left and people they don't like on the right. They could even be in the same position but one might be colour, one might be black and white, one might be fuzzy, one might be sharp. This might sound alien to people at the moment, but if you start tracking your pictures and noticing what things look like, you will notice their structure and how they are placed differently. It's just the way it works with the brain.

Strategies to Empower You

What is your current strategy in an area of life you want to be better or more effective in?

How do you think about it? What sort of thoughts do you have? What pictures come to mind? What do you say to yourself? Do you imagine other people saying things? Do you remember something someone else once said?

Whatever and however you are thinking, it is your strategy; and that current strategy generates a feeling inside you, one that either empowers you towards your goal or sends you running away from it, or, as is usually the case, somewhere in between the two extremes.

If your current strategy in a situation is not empowering you, then you need to change it to a more effective strategy; one that would generate more empowering emotions and lead to better actions and results.

Just think, if there's something where you aren't getting the end results you want, how are you thinking about it? What is your strategy?

Does your current strategy empower you or hold you back?

There are clues in everything you say if you're looking to work out what it is you are picturing in your mind, or what you might be saying to yourself.

Listen to the words you use because, quite often, the language you use tells of your inner experience. So if you say something like "I can't see myself doing it", that suggests you are either making pictures you don't believe or a picture of yourself failing. It tells you what elements are probably having the biggest impact on you at the moment. People will say things like, "It doesn't sound like the sort of thing I could do." That suggests the auditory part (they are either talking to themselves in their heads or remembering something someone else once said) of their strategy is having the most impact on them at the moment, when they're talking or thinking about it.

9

VISUALIZING FOR SUCCESS

How you visualize or imagine events or anything you do in life beforehand has a huge part to play in how well that experience goes.

I'm sure you must have been in a meeting or event where the outcome directly impacts your success. How you visualize these events beforehand not only determines how you behave, act and come across, but also how others will react to you in that environment.

Imagine you're going into a situation where beforehand you are thinking something like, "They're going to think I'm a right pest as soon as I get the catalogues out, they probably want to get on with other things, and are not interested in listening to what I have to say."

When you get there and they open the door, it doesn't matter how much you attempt to put on a fake, enthusiastic demeanour, something is not going to be right; there's going to be a disconnect – subconsciously it's not going to click right with them. We can detect so many things subconsciously from each other.

Imagine if you're thinking beforehand something like, "I'm going to go in there, I can't wait to show them these products, they're going to love the products."

You are making pictures of everyone looking at the catalogue, looking at the products and placing orders. When you go in there, you'll have genuine enthusiasm, which is one of the most contagious emotions. If you want people to be enthusiastic, you've got to be enthusiastic first. If you want people to be happy, you can't be sad and expect to be able to make someone else happy. So if you want people to be enthusiastic about what you are telling them or talking about, you've got to have passion and be enthusiastic.

I've met so many people that are so successful in selling and they tell me, "I'm lousy at sales, but I just love these products." (I know I said this earlier in the book, but some things are worth repeating.)

Your enthusiasm comes over and it makes everyone naturally think, "I'd better take a look at this!" It's not going to work with everyone, but if you go in without enthusiasm, you're not going to connect as well with the people there.

If it's a one-on-one situation, it's not so bad; you can get re-connected if you make a bad first impression. You can turn it around by talking about common interests, using common language styles, things like this, but you can't do this with eight or nine people in the room. Having said that, even in a one-to-one situation, there is no substitute for going in and making a great, enthusiastic first impression, this must always be your intention.

You have got to go in with enthusiasm and the expectation of a good outcome; it's one of the most important things because your expectation is based upon your beliefs. If you can't go into a situation with enthusiasm you need to ask yourself why not? What do you believe about that situation? Find out why you lack enthusiasm and do something about it.

One of the things we unfortunately do as humans is to think about our goals and where we want to be, hoping for success in the long term, yet expecting failure on a daily basis in the short term. That's the paradox, and the long term is after all an accumulation of all the "short terms" to come.

So your hopes come from your dreams and your wishes, whereas your expectations come from your beliefs. Unfortunately, your beliefs are stronger in most cases, so if you're expecting people not to be very welcoming, they won't be, whereas if you're expecting people to be friendly, they more likely will be. If you think about it, if you're going in to a group of people thinking they're not going to be friendly, you're going to feel and act differently than if you're expecting them to be friendly, so you can automatically self-fulfil what you're thinking about.

Of course, you're probably not going to take someone really, really miserable and make them really, really happy, in a first impression. You're going to impact it one way or the other and the chances are that it's going to be enough to help you get the outcome or results you are looking for.

It's really unfortunate that for most of us, if we are honest with ourselves, the biggest obstacle to our success is ourselves. It's almost as if you need to get out of your own way so you can move forward.

About ten years ago when I was still working in information technology, I went to a Direct Selling Association conference and my finance director, Maurice, came to me and said, "Mark, Mark, I've got brilliant news."

I asked, "What's that, what's that?"

He explained, "You can go on stage and do a two-minute presentation about our product."

I replied, "You're not getting me on stage!"

This was still the case five or six years ago, I was still dead scared about doing a presentation. I was fine with showing eight or so people through our software in a client demonstration or training, but as far as doing what I termed a proper talk in public to a group of people, I'd never do it. It was only through breaking down my strategies and applying what I am talking about here that I changed how I thought about things. Now I am at the stage where I get up and speak everywhere, all the time, and never even get nervous, because I changed how I thought about it. The main thing is I was expecting failure and thinking about speaking and everything going wrong! Once I started to think about it going well then, over time, it improved.

How you visualize things beforehand is so important with your expectations, because it is tied to the feeling of "I've already got it" as well, it is all the same sort of emotion.

One of the underpinnings of how we work is that every single resource, whether it's confidence, fear or whatever, we've all got them in us, we just don't use them in the right places. We've got wonky strategies, we've either attached the wrong emotion to something or the strategy we use is really out of date.

So, a quick little exercise:

Think about one of your strategies – start with something simple, something you either don't like very much or you procrastinate over doing.

First, I'll give you an example, one of my strategies, washing the car.

I'm going to wash the car, and I start to picture in my head the fact that I've got to sort out all the mess in the shed. Where did I put the sponge? I know I should have washed the sponge out last time. I'll have to find the hose, I don't know what the children have done with it after playing in the garden. When I wash the car, I'm going to get soaking wet, I won't be able to get it dry before it starts smearing, and it will probably be raining afterwards as well.

You know, if that's my strategy, it is very likely that I'll end up saying, "I can't be bothered to wash the car." Now imagine a different strategy. I think what it is going to be like after it's done, how good it's going to look, how good I'm going to feel that I've accomplished it. Now I'm more likely to do it.

One of the most powerful things with personal development and motivating yourself through anything, even if it's something you don't want to do, is to think how good it's going to feel five minutes after it's done, and picture yourself five minutes after. When you think about something you are not comfortable about and fear rises up, life seems to stop and your brain won't go beyond the event, it gets stuck in the fear. However, thinking about how good you'll feel later when it's over and you are doing things you enjoy is telling your brain that you do survive this and everything will be OK. This can often be enough motivation to move forwards.

I was working with someone recently who had to run a stall at an event. She was going to do this event last Christmas and she was really panicking about it. I told her to picture driving home afterwards, and think how good she would feel when it was finished. It worked, she felt better about it and whenever she thought of the upcoming event, she would leapfrog the actual event in her mind and focus on the journey home and what else she had to look forward to.

A lot of people who exercise a lot, who start going to the gym, or start exercising, think, "I can't be bothered to do this, it's so boring and so much effort, I can't be doing with that." You see these other people who go every day and you wonder how they do that, how do they go every day?

If you actually talked to them, a lot of them will tell you, "Yeah, it is a bit of a bind, but it's the feeling I get afterwards when I've done it. "

You have to get motivated by the outcome if it's a good thing, but if it's something you don't really want to do but need to, then you get motivated by how good you're going to feel when it's done and out of the way. You'll then focus on that more than the process of the thing you're going to go through. It's like in my example of washing the car. In my bad strategy, not only did I think of everything that could go wrong I also focused on all the steps involved. Whereas, once I had the good strategy I focused on the end result mainly and how great that would be.

Go ahead now and think about one of your strategies for something you either don't like very much or you procrastinate over doing, start with something simple, and remember:

As you think about it:

- What do you imagine happening?
- What sorts of feelings do you get?
- Do you say anything about it in your head?
- How does it sound inside your head, what tonality and speed is the inner voice?
- Do you remember something someone else once said?

Write it all down so you have a written record of your strategy for this aspect of your life.

If you find yourself saying you don't know the answers to these questions, then guess what they might be! Chances are you will be right; those guesses come from inside your mind, your own intuition based on your life experiences to date, your values and beliefs.

Once you've done that, think about the strategy you use for something you are really good at or really like doing.

As you think about it:

- What do you imagine happening, what sorts of feelings do you get?
- Do you say anything about it in your head?
- How does it sound inside your head, what tonality and speed is the inner voice?
- Do you remember something someone else once said?

Again, write this down.

Now you have two strategies written down, one where you are not very motivated and one where you are really motivated.

What do you think would happen if you took the thing you don't feel very motivated about or procrastinate over and used the strategy of the thing you are motivated to do?

So basically, think about the thing you don't like doing in the same way as you think about the things you do like doing, use the same speed and tonality of voice etc.

Why don't you have a go at that now?

Notice how you feel different about the thing you didn't feel that motivated to do. If you don't feel quite motivated or empowered to do it yet, then go back and double check the strategy that motivates you – have you missed a key step? Are you using the same pace and tonality for any internal voices?

Here's a good example of this: let's say you are looking forward to going on a great holiday. If you are like me, you probably daydream about what it's going to be like from time to time. When you daydream, what does the inner voice sound like? How do you picture things in your mind? Do you see yourself in the pictures you are making in your mind or are you viewing things as if through your own eyes? Perhaps that is a key part of your strategy or way of thinking about this area of your life.

Go back now, revise the strategy, then run it again against the thing you weren't very motivated to do . . .

Notice just how much better that feels now.

If you are not totally there yet, it could be an issue with your beliefs or comfort zone, which is what we are going to work on now!

10

THE COMFORT ZONE

The comfort zone is the playground of limiting beliefs. We don't want to think about stepping outside our comfort zone because people talk about it a lot that way and that can make us feel isolated and fearful.

I talk about expanding our comfort zone, you know taking baby steps, changing things, doing something different each day, just to push that comfort zone out further and to do something different. One of the things I say about fear is that most of the time when you are afraid, it's not whether you are going to get hurt or killed, it's a fear of what others might think: what if I look silly, what if I'm a nuisance, and all those sort of things. It's not a real fear. It feels real, but it's not because you know rationally when you're out of the situation that it's a silly thing to worry about. Very often you will convince yourself that next time you won't act like that again, but then you go into a similar situation and the fear surfaces automatically and you experience the fear again.

Think of fear or the fear signal you get as a traffic light system.

You've got red, amber and green; a lot of people go to the red stoplight as soon as they feel the fear.

Before a full-scale panic and retreat sets in, learn to see it as an amber light instead and make a decision. Think about it; is it something you really don't want to do, or do you actually wish deep down that you could do it? You know the situation where you tell yourself you want to do something and that other voice comes in, your inner critic, and reminds you or tells you that you can't do it or shouldn't do it because . . .

However, if it's something you really don't want to do, and both you and your inner voice agree, then go to red. Don't do it; you don't have to do anything you don't want to do.

If it's something you know deep down you want to do, perhaps it's one of those things where you wish you were different and could do it, then don't take that fear as a signal to *beware*, but take it as a signal to *be aware*. Be aware – this is something different or new and you need to pay attention, focus and apply any necessary skills to enable you to navigate through it and learn by the outcomes you get. Quite often, that fear signal is not really a fully-fledged fear, but an uncomfortable feeling because you don't have a pattern or strategy in your mind for approaching this particular activity with confidence.

It's like that driving lesson again. The one when you're sweating and thinking, "I'm not going to remember all this", it's just because you're not used to it, you've not done it before, or you've not done it enough times yet.

Take that fear as a signal to be aware, think "This is something new, I'm going to have to pay attention, it's going to feel uncomfortable until I get used to it."

The simplest things in life feel uncomfortable until you get used to them.

Here's a little exercise.

Cross your arms like many people do when relaxing.

Now cross them the other way round, without slipping back into the pattern of doing it the same way. You will most likely feel it's really uncomfortable. If you find it difficult, it's likely that you're so stuck in the autopilot pattern of the way you always fold them that you can't do it! So keep doing it until you manage to fold them the opposite way.

Why does it feel uncomfortable? Because you don't have a pattern or strategy internally that you are accustomed to for folding your arms this way; you're not used to it. You feel uncomfortable because you are not used to it.

The neural pathways in your brain are not used to this way of folding your arms. Does that mean this could never feel comfortable or normal? Of course not: if you did this enough, you'd get used to it and you'd be able to fold your arms both ways. You would develop a new pattern and you would feel comfortable with it. It's the same for anything you do, even those things currently outside your comfort zone. If you understand your strategy, adjust it where necessary, and apply it a number of times, then new patterns are formed and the fear signals fade away. You become comfortable doing things that previously caused distress and triggered the red light.

So everything has a pattern, all of our fears are patterns, and you either have to chip away at the limiting beliefs (covered in the next chapter), or change them, or get so much motivation that they pale into insignificance. How could that work?

Well, for instance, the fear of flying. Let's say someone has a fear of flying and they can't get on a plane. Yet, if someone puts a gun at their head, they'll get on a plane! Perhaps they just haven't got enough motivation in that example! It's so often not that we *can't* do things; it's that we *won't* do them. We will be looking at that very soon but, before we do, let's just finish up our thoughts on fear and the comfort zone.

So, take this "fear signal" that comes up when you are outside your comfort zone as a signal to be aware and not beware: that's what it's all about, the amber light. Once you are able to hold at the amber light and consider situations, you can then decide if you go to red and stop, or green and proceed.

Often, when you proceed, you still can feel some of that fear and carry on regardless.

Take, for instance, Jonny Wilkinson, the English rugby player; he's done a number of big kicks at the end of the game that will determine whether England wins or loses the World Cup. No pressure there then.

A radio interviewer asked him, "Jonny, do you ever get scared before you do those kicks?"

Jonny replied, "Yes, every time, but I know that fear is part of the process."

You need to realize that sometimes fear and feeling uncomfortable is part of the process if you're doing something different, no matter how simple it is, and knowing that can help you proceed from the amber light to the green light; from there, things can be so different.

Before we move on to looking at limiting beliefs, I want to remind you briefly about confidence and what I said earlier in this book.

People use the word confidence all the time without really thinking about what it is.

It's your degree of certainty about an outcome, about how you'll perform, how you'll feel in a situation; a lack of confidence means you've got an amount of uncertainty about a situation or the outcome. One of the keys, as I mentioned earlier, is expecting a good outcome by having a good way of thinking about it – a good strategy – or changing what you believe about yourself or a situation. Perhaps both a great strategy and changing some negative beliefs you may have.

Limiting Beliefs

Limiting beliefs are really just bad strategies, the person who sees a spider and panics, just has a bad strategy; the person who says, "I can't give presentations", "I can't make cold calls" or whatever, just has a bad strategy running in their head. If you think about it, most of these things we can see other people doing and the only thing that's different, if you've got the same skill knowledge, is just how you're thinking about it on a mindset level, your belief, confidence and motivation level.

So let's look at limiting beliefs, which are the beliefs we have about ourselves, what we need to do, the world in general, etc. that limit us from taking action or being the best we can be.

When we say things to ourselves, it can have a huge impact on how we feel about ourselves and our ability to progress and change.

For instance, if there is a situation where you keep getting results you don't like, you might be saying something like one of the following to yourself about it:

> **"Oh, I'm just stupid and don't know why I even attempt to do things."**

OR:

> **"I just don't know how to do this yet."**

Which of them would you most likely use?

It makes a huge difference to how your mind operates afterwards, and to the likelihood that you will ever be motivated to learn any new skills necessary.

So, quite often limiting beliefs can be changed if you attempt to force yourself through things; you find out you can do them. Likewise, even somebody else doing something can change your beliefs.

Quite often, if somebody else does something you don't believe is possible, it can give you the belief that maybe you can do it too.

It happened with the four-minute mile; no-one believed a human could run a mile in under four minutes. Then Roger Bannister did it and over the following twenty four months, six other people did it too. The belief was broken and others were then able to do what previously seemed, or was believed to be, impossible.

You can have personal beliefs about yourself and what you're capable of, and you can have global beliefs about people or the world in general.

"I can't speak in public" is a personal belief.

"Teenagers these days are all trouble" is a global belief.

"Money is the root of all evil" is also a global limiting belief.

A lot of people often don't appreciate these global limiting beliefs actually exist, but these common expressions heard all the time can be held at a subconscious level with people and it stops their progress.

I worked with a lady who was working for a large London legal firm. She was a senior manager who had an opportunity to become a partner but she said she couldn't go for it, something was holding her back. When we drilled down in this group session with her, we found out that she had two reasons. First, she had this image inside her mind like a banner saying, "I don't deserve success". It was going on inside her head, which wasn't really ideal, but it turned out it was something her mum had said to her at one stage. The other thing she had was this belief she had been taught as a young child that "Money was the root of all evil".

Now one way we can deal with global limiting beliefs when we notice them is this: if you say "Money is the root of all evil", it must mean that the opposite is also true, "The lack of money is the root of all good". Now we know that's not the case, so, when you do something like that, you can bring two beliefs together actually dispelling the original one and making them clash with each other because they conflict. Both beliefs can't be true so, therefore, perhaps neither are.

Limiting beliefs can impact your life so much and hold you back from doing things you could actually do if you changed those particular beliefs.

So you need to think about what the biggest obstacle to your success is; what is the biggest limiting belief that's holding you back? As I mentioned before, normally it's ourselves and something we believe about ourselves, or what we believe about something we're going to do.

One of the things we need to do is to get back to being more like young children, because our brains love stories and we love pretending. That's how we learnt when we were young;

you may remember my bigheaded bookstore visualization in Part One. So if there are calls you don't like making, then go pick the phone up, keep your hand on the receiver and pretend you're making a call.

It sounds stupid, but it helps. You get different emotions attached to the action of going over and picking up the phone, which at the moment has got some fear emotion, and you can start to chip away at that if you get used to taking the action in a non-fearful way. You can change the association; or find a bit of music that really makes you feel empowered or feel good, play it, and then go and make the call. Dial while the music is playing and just as they answer, pause the music. That sort of thing can easily flip over your emotional state to get you to do that thing; then you should find, after you've done it a few times, you start to associate different feelings with that experience. In NLP terms, this is called an "anchor", something that links you back to an emotion or memory with an associated emotion.

On one occasion, before I had finally overcome my own fear of public speaking, I was scheduled to be on stage to speak to a large audience one Sunday morning. All day Saturday I was all right. However, when I woke up on Sunday morning, all I could think was "I can't do this, there's no way I can do this! What am I going to say? I know, I'm ill . . . no, what am I going to say?"

All these negative thoughts of doom went through my mind, but I had to put the brakes on and say, "Stop, hold on, slow down, there is a part of you Mark that wants to be able to do this, that would love to be able to do this."

I basically thought, "I'm going to have to do something". So, I got my MP3 player, put on some music that made me feel I could do anything, and it really worked. After about ten minutes, not only was I exhausted from jumping around the hotel room like a lunatic, I was ready to go and do the talk. However, I realized one important thing – and this is important about so many things in life – you have to break the patterns that lead to these emotions.

You see how I used music there to change my state. At the time, I was in such a panic that I didn't have time to start thinking about some of the things we're going to explore in the next chapters. I just knew that I quickly needed to change my emotions and so I found music was the quickest way; a quick fix.

Shortly, we will learn an easy process to start breaking down those limiting beliefs where you say you can't do something. First though, let's take a look at that inner voice and the language we use when we talk to ourselves in our thoughts.

We want to use that voice as an inner coach as opposed to the inner critic that it tends to be for most of us if we don't train it properly.

11

INNER CRITIC TO INNER COACH

One of the big things to look at is how to "talk to yourself" when moving on from what could be called "bad outcomes". An example is if you've done something and it hasn't gone very well, or as well as you had expected.

What we tend to do in these situations is to use "modal operator" words. There are words of necessity and possibility, for example:

Necessity	Possibility
Can't	Won't
Should	Could
Must	Might

"Should" is an interesting one because it is different for different people, and what I mean by this is when some people say they *should* do something, they do it, yet for others, the word doesn't have enough commitment and they need to be saying *must* or *will*.

What that means is if you say to yourself, "I should make that call today", do you usually do it?

So, *should* is used in different ways by different people as mentioned earlier. When you come out of an event or a meeting, for example, and it hasn't gone very well, you might start saying to yourself something like, "I should have done this; I should have said that, I should have said the other". This is very often delivered in a downward "beating ourselves up" type of tonality.

In this situation, you concentrate on what went wrong; and actually build a picture in your mind of what went wrong. What you're basically doing then is building yourself up more and more towards never doing it again!

There are two things that need to be done if this is an activity that you would really like to get better at, or would like to have gone better at the time:

1) Change the "should" to a "could" and say, "I could have done this, I could have done that".

2) Use a more upbeat tonality because the words don't always make that much difference, it's the tonality that gives language meaning, not the words.

For example, if you were to say "Get out of here" to someone who just said something quite amazing or a juicy bit of gossip, or you had just been really annoyed by someone and wanted them to leave you alone and you screamed, "Get out of here", we have the very same words but completely different meaning. This is because of the tonality and volume of the voice used; it's the same with that voice in your head, it's got tonality too. "I should have done this, I should have done that", comes with a telling off tonality, whereas, "I could have done this or I could have done that" can be used with an encouraging, "I've got a new idea" type of tonality. This should make you feel quite different.

The tonality is the most important thing because when you're using the upbeat, encouraging tonality, you're making pictures in your mind of doing it again. You're thinking of new ideas, different ways of doing it. You're not saying, "I screwed up because I didn't do this last time." You are saying, "Oh, I've found a way I can use next time, a different approach, you know, I've got some new ideas, that could give me better results next time."

However, the reason I advise people to not just take "should" and apply the upbeat tonality, even though I just said the tonality was the main thing, is because should is a funny word, as I said. It varies from person to person, but the word should has got an element of guilt attached to it and guilt is not a useful emotion.

If you compare "should have done that" with "could have done this", you will notice a different emotional tug. It might be a big tug; it's different for different people, but those little emotions are what we respond to on a daily basis, usually outside of our conscious awareness, and they make us decide if we do or don't feel good about something.

So, ideally, you need to change the *should* to *could*, and apply the more upbeat "I've got a great idea for next time" type of tonality. This is when the inner voice becomes an inner coach rather than an inner critic.

The "I can't" Virus

You may remember that the top of the lists of words of necessity and possibility in the previous section were the words can't and won't.

Now with can't and won't, when people say "I can't do something", in most cases that means that they "won't do it because . . ." What follows the "because" is a fear, a phobia, some imagined consequence or some limiting belief.

It's all too often not that they can't do it, it's that they won't, but because for so long they've said "I can't do it" they have linked it to their identity. By saying can't, they don't even venture to imagine what it would be like to do whatever it is.

If you don't imagine it, you won't do it, so what you need to do is change the way you are thinking about it.

How you think about things has a massive impact on how they turn out. For instance, you could have two people, one gets on and makes sales calls and the other just can't do it. Now there can only be one real difference between these two people – how they are thinking about it!

Can't says I have never been able to, and I never will be able to, it's not bound by time or anything, it just says I can't. When you say "I won't do it", you've actually made the choice not to. You've got a choice, you're just deciding not to do it because of some fear, usually, or some imagined consequence.

"I can't" says to your brain you never have been able to so you never will be able to – "it's just the way I am!" So you don't tend to allow your brain to look for potential solutions.

The "I can't" in most cases usually means:

"I won't do X because of Y."

The other thing you can do yourself, or say to other people if they say they can't do something, is to add the word "yet" to the end of the statement.

Yet is such a powerful word because it assumes that you will do it one day! It doesn't mean you are going to go and do it right away, but you've made a slight shift because you probably never saw yourself doing it before. By just adding "yet" on the end, you now can.

So you need to change the belief when you say you can't do things. One way to do that is by breaking down the belief and understanding it, or by getting enough emotional blackmail, or a good enough reason to get on with doing it. In life you'll find that you will do anything if you have a good enough reason. Remember the example of how someone with an extreme phobia of flying would get on a plane if their life depended on it?

To break down and understand the belief and develop emotional blackmail on ourselves, you can ask yourself a series of questions to change "can't" to "won't".

Go ahead and pick one now to work on; what is it for you? What do you find yourself saying you can't do? Is it:

- "I can't speak in Public."
- "I can't sell."
- "I can't delegate."
- "I can't speak to people I don't know."

Now you have one, let's work on it.

Question 1: "How do you know you can't?"

When I ask, "How do you know you can't" the response very often is, "I just can't."

I follow it up with, "No, seriously, I'm interested; how do you know you can't, I want to know."

They typically then go to one of two positions.

"I've never done it before."

Well that doesn't mean they can't do it, does it? They've just never done it before. They might need more skill knowledge, to know how to do it, when to do it, whatever, or they might need more belief, confidence or motivation. Never having done it, however, doesn't mean they can't do it.

Another common response is:

"I did it once and it worked out badly or it went wrong."

Well that doesn't mean they can't, because they actually did it once! They just didn't get the outcome they wanted. So did they have unrealistic expectations, or do they simply need more skill knowledge, or more belief, or more confidence?

Sometimes, it can be unrealistic expectations. If you've made two or three phone calls and people said no so you give up, then you're going to find out from the experts that the best people only tend to get three or four out of ten, maximum, to say yes. Look at the top sports people; they get paid thousands a week, but do they score every time they kick the ball at the net? No, they probably score one in thirty shots and they get paid thousands a week for "failing" most of the time.

It's easy to get hung up because of school and having our errors pointed out to us, we get so hung up as soon as we get something that doesn't work out, but we need to understand that it may not work the first time.

You're going to find that everyone's different, not everyone is going to want what you're offering, and they aren't necessarily saying no to you. They may not be ready for it, they may not realize what's good for them, but so often, it's unrealistic expectations that make people stop doing things and say they can't or they say they have failed.

We need to expect to win every time we go into a situation with enthusiasm and on the occasion it doesn't happen we realize it is an unplanned outcome as discussed in Part One.

It gets worse when the economy goes through an apparent slow period. Someone will think, "I'm going to have an event, I'm going to phone someone, see if they want to come to an event." They'll make the first phone call and the people say they will be on holiday; "Well, they said they're on holiday but it might be because of the economy". They'll phone the next person and they'll say they're doing something, and don't want to be involved. "Oh, I reckon it is the economy", is the thought after that call and by the time the third person has said no, even though they might all be valid reasons, there is a risk of us believing it now *is because of the economy* and what's the point!

The trouble is, as soon as you get to that situation you start changing your behaviour, you start to believe it's futile. "I was going to make some other calls but there's no point is there? They're telling me on the news, there's no point, I might as well not bother." You may not realize but you start to change what you're doing and manifest the very thing you fear.

Question 2: What really prevents you from doing this?

In the first question, you're looking for evidence. What's the evidence for you saying you can't do something?

"What really *prevents* you" is looking for the consequences; what would be the consequences of doing this that are stopping you from doing it?

This is going to bring out the fears and the things you worry about, what you think might happen.

Just make a big list, keep writing down everything you believe might happen, or could happen, or you've heard happen to someone else.

"What really prevents you" gets the fears and the consequences out into the open.

What can sometimes happen at this stage is that people look at what comes up on these lists and can't believe some of the silly reasons and fears there; things that may apply as a child, but in no way apply as an adult. It's just without awareness of what is running automatically in our heads; we just accept the negative emotion generated by thoughts usually outside our awareness and retreat from these situations.

Question 3: What positives would it mean to your life if you could do this?

So this thing you don't want to do, or you don't think you can do, what would happen if you could do it?

What positives would it mean to your life and those around you?

For example:

"I'd be more successful."

"I'd build a better life for myself."

"I'd realize my ambitions."

"I'd be able to take the children on a better holiday."

Now add as much emotional blackmail as you can get on yourself to the upside if you did this thing; you want all the blackmail you can get on yourself and then . . .

Question 4: What negatives would it mean to your life if you never do this?

List what will happen if you don't ever master this, the negatives.

For example:

"I'll always wonder if I ever reached my full potential."

"Will I wonder if I could have achieved more in life?"

"I won't be able to do the things I want to do for my children."

"I'll never make enough money to really enjoy life and have peace of mind."

Get all that good negative stuff that's going to motivate you.

You don't have to tell people to do the above two questions, they do it automatically, but they do it the other way round. They think of the positives of not doing something, such as, "I won't have to go through it, I won't have to face it." Then they think of the negatives of doing it; "If I do it, I might feel scared, if I do it they might have a go at me." People do it the wrong way round, you've got to flip it and think of all the positives if you were to do this thing you say you can't do, and all the negatives if you don't ever do it.

Once you make these lists and you read through them, you'll find out that one of these lists might feel more motivating to you than the other, and what you've discovered in that context is your motivation strategy.

You see, with our motivation, we can either use a "motivated towards" or a "motivated away" from strategy.

For instance, take two people both in the same bad financial situation, both want to be really rich. One person could motivate themselves by thinking how good it's going to be when they get really rich and all the things they'll do – they're motivating themselves towards the good outcome. The other person is saying, "Right, I couldn't bear to have the bailiffs come round, or have the house re-possessed." They're motivating themselves by getting away from the bad outcome, so there's a difference, and that's what these last two questions were looking at.

The first was a "motivated towards" question and the second was a "motivated away from" question. I suggest that if one of them feels better than the other, or feels more motivating for you, then drop the other list and just focus on the one that works better.

So whenever you can think of the positive outcome you want and not the negative you don't want. You know the subconscious mind is what is controlling you and it can't process negatives; only the conscious mind can process the negative and apply it afterwards, and then it's too late. Don't think of a tropical island, too late you've just thought of one!

Real-life Examples

I went to see the bank manager and, in the general chit chat, she asked me, "Are you still doing those talks?" I said I was, and she continued, "You know what my problem is, I can't delegate."

I said, "You mean you *won't* delegate."

She went, "Oh yes, actually you're right." Her understanding of the situation changed in an instant.

Just that simple thing and she's thinking about it differently because when I said "you won't", she started to think about it. "Well, why, won't I? It's true I won't, so why won't I?" She then starts to think people will think she is putting on them, they'll think she is lazy, why can't she do it herself, or whatever else it is that runs through her mind. She then starts to realize why she's built this belief and once you realize that, you can start to get some power over it and change it.

I had this guy who told me, "You know, I really want to start my own business, but I'd be so disappointed if I start it and it doesn't work out. I don't think I'd be able to handle the disappointment."

I replied, "Okay then, let's fast forward fifty years, you're ninety years old, you're looking back on your life, and you've never started your own business, how do you feel."

There was a pause and he answered, "Oh, disappointed." He even used the same words!

So I told him, "Okay, you've got two options, one is you start your own business and you might be disappointed, the second one is you don't start your own business and you will be disappointed, which seems the bigger risk?"

He said I was right. It worked for him; he changed in that instant and went on to start his own business.

For some people, it will work in the short term but not long term because you're talking about a downside far off in the future. One of Tony Robbins' big things is saying that we won't go through short-term pain for long-term gain, that's the big thing we've got to get over, that's why those questions about the positives of doing it help. We're looking to get over short-term pain for long-term gain.

So, I always say, imagine you're looking back in years from now at the opportunities you didn't take, what would that feel like then?

Another example: I had someone in direct selling who wanted to recruit more people into her team tell me, "I can't sell to or recruit strangers, I don't like being around strangers."

That's such a common one. The trouble with using the word "strangers" is that it starts with the word "strange", and the subconscious processes it as strange, which isn't going to help much! I say to people, think of them as people we've not yet met, people we don't yet know. They often reply with, "Isn't that a bit fluffy?" Well, it is a bit fluffy, but it feels a lot better.

The other thing I say to people is that if you think about people other than your immediate family (who were forced upon you!), everybody else in your life that's given you a job, given you a pay rise, made you laugh, made you smile, you've fallen in love with, whatever, they were all strangers once so there must be some more good ones out there!

Our biggest opportunities for even more success and happiness in life lies with the people we don't yet know.

Belief Conflicts

So, this brings us to belief conflicts.

When I owned my own business, it was quite a small business. By the end we had fourteen employees but we started with one – me. The next day we made it two when I hired my cousin Steven as a trainee, so pretty much everything still came down to me.

I even had to make the cold calls to sales prospects and I hated making those calls to people to see if they were interested in talking about our software.

The reason I didn't like making the cold calls is I thought that the person on the receiving end had control because they were going to decide if they were interested or not. They were going to make me happy or sad, they were in control and I didn't like it.

Then, when I got home at night and the phone used to ring and it was a withheld number, I thought, "I'm not going to answer that because it might be someone trying to sell me something." I'd feel that if I answered it, I wouldn't be able to say no and I wouldn't be able to put the phone down, and I might end up buying something I didn't want.

So in that situation, I was saying to myself that the person who's making the cold call has got control. At that point, I realized this was a belief conflict; both can't be true so perhaps neither are, and it fell away.

12

THE POWER OF THOUGHTS

The thing with thoughts is we become them, or we become what we think about most of the time.

Where you are today is the sum total of all the thoughts that you've had. If you remember thoughts, feelings, actions, outcome, they all start with thoughts. So what you've thought up until now has got you to where you are today. That's a fact and all you need to realize is that the same thing is happening on a second-by-second basis. When you think a limiting belief thought or a negative thought that's affecting your outcome, feelings and your actions, it is actually pre-building the future of where you are going to be. These thoughts mean the things you keep putting off will have a major impact in the long term on where you're going to end up!

Most people seriously underestimate the impact our thoughts have on our results. I said earlier, because of the on-going cycle of thoughts, feelings, quality of action and outcome, we need to change our thinking and how we are thinking to change our outcomes or results.

The other thing about thoughts is that what dominates your thoughts also influences your results; you need to be aware of that: the things you think about most are affecting your results.

Now this is where it gets really, really interesting. You've got to start thinking about what you're thinking about! We think on two levels, we can ask ourselves, "Why do I think that?" "Why am I saying that?" "Why do I feel like this in this situation?" We need to start thinking about what we are thinking about.

When you get a negative emotion over something you are thinking about doing, or are currently doing, you need to think, "Well, why am I thinking that?" You need to be aware of what you are thinking because these thoughts run on autopilot. You just think about doing something, you get the emotion, you don't do it and you go on to do something else instead. You can start to slow it down and find out what the strategy is, "What am I saying to myself, what am I picturing?" Then you can change these things and break them down; it's the skill knowledge and mindset aspect of thoughts.

You also need to ask better questions of yourself, by applying this next concept I am about to explain.

When attempting to do something, you might say to yourself things like:

"I'm never going to think of a way to do this."

"I can't think of a way to do this."

"There's no way of doing this."

You are shutting off so much brain processing power because all your brain is doing is reinforcing not doing it, not doing it, no way, no way, it's manifesting it.

If you just break that cycle and ask yourself,

"What could make this work?"

"What could make this better?"

your brain will start to find answers. They may not come up immediately, you may go out to the shops and suddenly something will spring into your mind, but if you find there's something you're struggling with and you think there's no answer, there's no way, no solution, you should actually stop yourself and say:

"What could make this work?"

"What would make this better?"

"What haven't I done yet?"

"What haven't I thought of yet?"

You'll start to notice things, you'll start to get answers. It comes from a Henry Ford saying that you need to remind yourself of:

"Whether you believe you can or you can't, you're usually right."

If there is something I don't want to do or I don't feel very good about doing, I say to myself, "How would I feel and what would I be thinking if I was totally motivated to do this and was excited about doing this?"

This helps me to build the pictures and feelings of how I would think and feel if it was something I felt good about doing, it helps me to build a new strategy.

I'd say to myself, "What would someone who really was into doing this think, what sort of things would they be picturing, what sort of things would they say to themselves?"

It helps you to step outside your own map of the world for a minute to build a new way of thinking about something. The other way is to identify a belief or a limiting belief that is holding you back.

Sometimes you may not have any idea about the thoughts or beliefs that might be holding you back. So start from the end point, the emotion you are feeling about it, and ask yourself:

"What must I believe in order to feel like this, what must I believe about myself, other people or the world in general?"

This might sound silly, but, if you do it, you'll find it works. For example, say you don't like going to talk to people you don't know. When you think about doing it, you get a really bad feeling, and tell yourself, "I don't want to do it." At that point you should then ask yourself:

"Well, what must I believe in order to feel like this?"

151

You might get answers like:

"I'm not good enough."

"They might not want me talking to them."

"They might have a go at me."

The beliefs will start to come out. If you ask yourself, you can answer yourself!

"What must I believe in order to feel like this?" This helps you get back to the belief level to realize what these limiting beliefs are, and then you can apply the questions that we spoke about earlier on in this book.

13

FINAL "THOUGHTS"

If you do the same things, you get the same results. Some people go to the same supermarket every day because they know where everything is. Why not go to a different super-market, you're going to have to find where the things are; it might seem like a pain, but you're going to grow new neural pathways. Drive a different way to work, it makes you focus and think more; all the time you're thinking more, you're growing and you're not on autopilot.

If you tap the back of your hand with the index finger of the other hand, it hurts at first, but after a while you don't feel it; the nerves get bored, they get used to the pattern, it goes numb and you don't feel it any more.

Some people go to the same holiday destinations every year because it's comfortable; they know what to expect, but they seriously cut off their range of emotions.

If you go somewhere different, you're going to get different emotions; you're going to build new neural pathways. If you're not moving forwards, you're moving backwards; there's no standing still. The human mind and the brain are designed like plants to grow and move forwards. If you don't move forwards, you move back.

Some people say, "Well, I stand still." They don't stand still, they take a step forward and a step back, a step forward and a step back, it seems like they're standing still but they're not really.

We all hear these stories, about the person who's ninety-five years old, gets up every day, does their own crosswords, does their own garden, still very active, and then you read about the someone else who retired at fifty-five and after a couple of months, it's all over because they didn't do anything but watch TV all the time, they just deteriorated.

So the minute you're not using your brain, you deteriorate. We all know the definition of insanity; it is doing the same thing over and over and expecting a different result. It doesn't work, and, as I said earlier, remember to think about what you're thinking about.

Instead of running away when a fear feeling or bad feeling comes up, get curious about it, ask yourself what must you believe in order to feel like that, then go about changing that belief.

Remember the three most important things covered in this book:

1. It's essential to think about your dream life and feel what it will feel like when you are living it for real. That "already achieved it" feeling.
2. What you may previously have called "failure" is really an "unplanned outcome".
3. "Can't" is usually "won't".

So, what's now stopping you moving forwards? Is it your "one thing"? I believe at any point in time that there is always "one thing" that we believe more than anything else that is stopping us from taking our life to the next level.

Let me finish by helping you get your one thing into perspective.

My final words, something to think about, your "one thing"

As I mentioned in the previous section, through the thousands of people I have spoken to about success and living their dream lives, most seem to have this one thing, this wall or barrier that they believe if it wasn't there, they would be moving to the next level.

For some I have worked with, their one thing has been something like speaking in public, making sales calls, talking to people they don't know, and many other things that are in fact actions they don't want to take.

When I ask people why they don't want to take them, fear is an answer I get a lot of the time, or thinking the other people may disapprove, or say "No".

There seems to be a common thread in wanting to avoid disappointment, rejection or failure. After all, you are not putting off doing your one thing because you think it might go really well, are you?

Many people seem to be plagued by a fear of things not working out or of getting something wrong. We just don't want to be disappointed.

One of the biggest thrills you can get in life is the emotion of how great you feel when you achieve something or win at something that shows how far you have come. There has to be the risk of not achieving or not winning in order for it to be so special when you do.

How can you really feel like you achieved something if it was so easy to achieve? How could you win and be over the moon if it was so easy to win? You couldn't.

Take the traditional board games like Ludo, Snakes and Ladders or Monopoly. If you knew you would win every time you were going to play those games, what would it be like? It would be fun at first but after a while it would get boring, and you wouldn't want to play anymore.

So achievement and winning is so special when you achieve and win something for the first time, something at the next level in business or as a person.

So what if you don't win or you don't achieve? Sure, you may be a little disappointed in that moment, but you know you haven't failed, right? After all, it is an unplanned outcome. You still have the opportunity to do it again, but perhaps in a different way, with different people, and win and achieve on a future occasion.

You will recall from the very early chapters that failure is to be seen as an unplanned outcome, and you only fail when you decide not to go for your goal or dream anymore. Failure is in your control.

At the end of the day, you might find that you'll often still come back to this worry about things not working out.

I observe human behaviour a lot and a sight I often see when I am out and about, perhaps walking or driving, is an elderly person in their eighties or nineties in their houses looking out of the window at the world going by. Most of the time they have moved their chair in front of the window so they can sit there for hours at a time, just watching.

What are they thinking? Well, I know what most of them are thinking because I've asked a number of people who do this. Most of them are thinking about what they would do differently if they had their time again.

The human brain plays a funny trick on us as we get older. The older we get, the less we worry about what others might think or the fact we might get something wrong or lose at something.

When these people get into their older years, they realize much too late that all the stupid things they worried about when they were younger, like the fact someone may say no, they might get something wrong or they may fail, were, in the grand scheme of life and living, **totally insignificant**.

You have the opportunity here and now to realize that and to move on and take those actions so you will be looking back and smiling and thinking, "Wow, what a ride" rather than "I wish I had . . ."

So when you think about your one thing that would take your life to the next level, don't keep putting it off saying, "Next year I'll do it." Otherwise, very soon all the next years will bring you to your own chair in your very own window of regret.

Because it's not about next year, or next month, or next week, it's not even about next time.

I want to leave you with these thoughts:

What about now?
What about today?

How I Became Successful – Mark's Story

When I speak to audiences about success, I usually start by asking a lot of questions and then answering them myself.

The funny thing is, this so-called "introduction" can last for half an hour. What the audience don't realize is that a lot of the principles, learning and tips that follow are embedded in this opening exchange.

You see, we are learning all the time, whether we realize it or not. In fact, if you don't take more control over what you learn you can learn some pretty unhelpful things.

None of us are strangers to this. From a young age we become experts at learning things that are no use to us – and in some instances things that can seriously affect our future success.

Take school, for instance. One bad experience reading aloud in class can live with you forever. The emotions attached to your experience teach you that speaking out loud is a scary thing to do. Many years later and guess what? You're still scared of doing it and now it has a name; "fear of public speaking".

The first question I put to my audience is:

"How did I get to be where I am today?"

Well, every time I thought about doing something different in my career, it happened – even totally changing careers a number of times.

After about four or five years in accounting, and that many jobs later, I started to think about how great it would be to work in computers. By then I was well into my twenties, and didn't know how I'd achieve this; I just knew how good it would be to be living that life. I basically started to daydream like a four year old.

Four year olds live in the moment, don't care what others might think, or that things may not work out, and they keep at something until they master it. If you think about it, how much more successful and happy would we be in our lives if we lived in the moment, didn't worry about the past or the future, didn't get worried about what other people might think and kept going at things until we could master them? Just like a four year old.

So, throughout this book, I have not really asked you to learn anything new. In fact, I've asked you to unlearn all the rubbish and limitations that stop you being the best you can be, that you too have most likely picked up since you were four years old. You see, you were also that four year old once.

Anyway, as I was well into my twenties by now, I didn't know how I'd achieve this; I just knew how good it would be to be living that life. In the daytime I was physically working in accounting, but in my head I was constantly thinking how my life would be if I was working in computers. I would imagine myself meeting new people, travelling the world, earning lots more money and buying all the cars I'd dreamed of. I would imagine what I would feel like, the things I would do, the types of people I would meet and how my friends and family would talk to me about my new career in computers.

A period of probably six months passed, and I was in another accounting role, when an opportunity came up to get involved in an IT project.

After about a year, I started to daydream again and think about how great it would be to work freelance and visit different clients during the course of a week. So, again I would constantly daydream about what my life would be like once I was working freelance. I'd take days off when I wanted, go on holiday when I wanted and have a great variety in my working week looking after all my clients.

A little while later, I got made redundant and was then given the opportunity to work on a project on a temporary basis. "Right", I thought, "this isn't a temporary job; this is my first client as a freelancer."

At this point in time, I thought I was just lucky in bringing to life all my dreams. But, I'd just accidentally, without realizing it, discovered how to use my brain to guide me towards opportunities and ideas I wouldn't normally notice, and then enabled me to take advantage of them. I learnt that the way you look at things greatly affects your ongoing experience, where you can start getting even better results in your own life. When I say your "own life" this is true – this doesn't have to just be about business or financial success, the same process and technique works for any aspect of your life. About five years ago I was asked to speak at a conference about success. I didn't tell the audience this was for business success – and, therefore, what happened actually surprised me. The audience consisted of 250 people, 246 were women and as a result of that talk three women decided to leave their husbands! All the time I was teaching the audience how to imagine their ideal life, and for these three women, it meant their husband wasn't in them!

Anyway, back to the point where I had become freelance. I loved being freelance, never in the same place for very long, the occasional project working from home, travel, not tied to the same office building day in and day out. I was earning more money in a month than most of my friends earned in a year. But then it happened again – I started to think how great it would be to own my own company with staff, a software product and all that goes with owning my own business. Yes, I was back to those very detailed daydreams picturing what my life would be like on a daily basis, the sorts of things I'd do – I'd even imagine being on holiday and how I would be thinking back to the previous few years with a booming software business.

You can guess by now what I'm going to write next; yes, an opportunity came along. I had been working freelance with this company for about eighteen months, when I was asked by the financial director to put a proposal together and attend a meeting with himself and the managing director.

In the meeting the managing director took the proposal document from me, and just put it to one side. "I have three questions for you Mark" he said:

"Will this do what we want?"

"Yes", I said.

"Are you confident you can do this?"

"Yes", I said.

"How much will it cost?"

"£150,000 but you need to give me £35,000 to get started", I said.

The managing director said, "Let's do it."

Those three questions have always stuck in my mind:

"Will this do what we want?"

"Are you confident you can deliver this?"

"How much will it cost?"

This is not just because it led to my first order as a software company owner. A little while later, I realized the true significance and meaning of those three questions and the order they were asked.

Price was the last thing they were interested in. First, they wanted to know if it would do what they wanted, and whether I could deliver it. Only *then* were they interested in the price. So many times I have mentored businesses that get so hung up on price. If sales are down, they assume that their prices are too high. The biggest issue though, I find, with businesses and price is they don't aim their product or service at a specific market or market segment. Nor do they market with an appropriate message to that segment. So, price often isn't the issue; it is usually that the business isn't demonstrating the value of their offering correctly.

For example, take a ball point pen. You can buy one in a regular office supplies store for about £1 or you could buy one in a Jewellery shop in Bond Street, London for £10,000 or more. They both do the same thing, but they are aimed at different markets and marketed in different ways.

So there I was, running my own software company, now working on some very big projects with some very large companies. Things couldn't get any better so you'd have thought by now that that would be enough for me.

However, that's the funny thing with us humans; we need to keep growing, moving forwards and progressing if we thrive on that feeling of success and of achieving something at one time we couldn't do.

So yes, I started to think and dream again, this time about how great it would be to sell my business and achieve that common significant title given to people who have a certain value of assets. Two years later, I achieved this, and it was at this point that I really started to think, "Wow, how did all that happen?"

I couldn't believe all this had happened to me, and started to become curious about success. I wanted to find out what makes a person successful, and more importantly what had made me successful.

I started doing a lot of research and began a quest to understand the "success mindset".

I signed up for a three-month course in a hypnotherapy clinic to see at source how the brain works, why we behave differently from each other, and answer many other unsolved questions. I wanted to understand how I had made these massive changes myself, because if I understood how, perhaps I could then make more use of this ability.

I remember thinking how fantastic the course was within the first twenty minutes on the first day. I loved what I had heard already, had a genuine interest in the subject and, as you now know, having genuine enthusiasm and passion are things that make us perform to our best and love every minute of it.

Every week at the clinic we had to work with real live clients that came in – and they'd come in with everything under the sun. There were people who wanted to stop smoking, a fear of motorway driving, spider phobias, fear of heights, a lady who couldn't stop eating toilet rolls and even a woman with a fear of wooden floors!

After a while, I came across another technology, or way of looking at things, called NLP – Neuro Linguistic Programming – which I now call "Common Sense Written Down".

I went to study with Richard Bandler, who, along with John Grinder, "formulated" the ideas behind NLP.

In the early seventies, Richard Bandler and John Grinder realized that some therapists were actually getting amazing results just by talking to people and bringing about rapid change. They wondered how this was being done, so they started to study and breakdown everything these therapists were doing.

A lot of it was to do with the actual *language* the therapists were using, and as NLP stands for "Neuro *Linguistic* Programming", it stood to reason.

By studying and modelling these expert therapists, they worked out how the brain works in terms of thoughts, feelings, things we say to ourselves, pictures we make in our heads and all those sort of things.

Following this, I decided to go on a "licensed trainer" course to get some more exposure to the ideas and learn some advanced aspects of personal development. However, going on this course meant I'd have to deal with one of my own fears in the process – speaking in public! Now my fear about speaking in public was something that had stayed with me all through owning my own business and beyond. When you own your own business, no one else can tell you what to do, and so if there was ever an opportunity to speak, I could always get out of it.

However, there was no getting out of it on this course – I was now going to have to speak for a minute in front of 100 people every day. What made it seem worse was that you'd be speaking to your peers, those who were also learning to be trainers. This was a big step so I employed a "coping process" to make it happen.

Firstly, I told myself that I would book the course, but I didn't *have* to go – I could choose to pull out if I wanted to.

When it got to the first day, I told myself I would drive there but I didn't have to go in – I could turn round and come home at any point. Then once there I told myself I could go in and register, but if I didn't like anything I could just go home. I went into the first session knowing if anything started to happen I didn't like I could slip out to the toilet and run home! I stayed and pushed through each of those stages.

Following this, I then judged my progress on the nine-day course, by whether I had breakfast or not. On the first day, I had no breakfast, on the second day, no breakfast, on the third day, I had a bit of toast, and by the end of the course, I was eating a full English breakfast! That's how I measured my progress.

One of the problems most people seem to have when attempting new things is they don't have a measure to track their progress. I tracked mine in stages, I'd booked, I'd left home to get there, I'd gone in, I'd stayed the first day and then I went into the breakfast analysis I have just mentioned.

Even if I had simply got to the venue on the first day, and then turned around and gone straight home, I would still have counted this as progress. Previously I would never have even got to the stage of booking on such a course, let alone turn up! So progress, no matter how small, was celebrated every small step along the way.

Not long after the courses one of my previous clients asked what I'd been up to. They then invited me to speak at their conference and that was the start of many talks for them and other companies who wanted their people to adopt a success mindset.

After a while, I decided I wanted to do my own events where there would be less restriction on time. Doing my own events also gave me the opportunity to start developing my own products, one of which includes this book. *Think Your Way to Success* came about because after a three-hour "Success Mindset" talk, many members of the audience had asked if there was anything more to take away than just the notes they managed to jot down.

After my talks, which became more and more popular, the audience members started to ask me to go into their businesses and work with them and their staff. This led to me becoming a mentor as well as a speaker, helping those businesses to have more success in all areas.

For more information, go to my website at www.rhodes2success.com where you can find out about the events I'm speaking at and sign up for my regular newsletter of Success and Personal Development.

There are also details on my website about my work as a speaker and business mentor around the world and how to get in touch with me, or you can find me on Twitter: @rhodes2success and Facebook: www.facebook.com/markrhodes2success. There is also a Facebook page at www.facebook.com/thinkyourwaytosuccess.

I wish you every success for the future.

Mark.

mark@rhodes2success.com

Index